The LLC & S-Corp Beginner's Guide

(2 Books In 1)

A Complete Guide On Forming Your Limited
Liability Company & S Corp, Plus Small
Business Taxes & Tips

By

Garrett Monroe

Buyer Bonus

As a way of saying thank you for your purchase, we're giving you our *"7-Figure Business Toolkit"* that includes five FREE downloads that are exclusive to our book readers!

Here's what you'll get:

1. **The Negotiation Mastery Cheat Sheet** – Master the art of negotiation and get a massive edge in your business.

2. **The Start Your LLC Checklist** – This step-by-step PDF shows you exactly how to get your LLC up and running right away.

3. **The Top 7 Websites To Start Your LLC** – Save hours on research and choose the best website to start your LLC.

4. **The Mindfulness Hacks for Entrepreneurs PDF** – Stay cool, calm, and collected through all the ups and downs of your business journey.

5. **The 5 Mistakes Beginners Make When Opening an LLC** – An email course that helps you avoid the most COSTLY mistakes when getting started.

To download your 7-Figure Business Toolkit, you can go to

https://llclegend.com/llc-s-corp-bonus **or simply scan the QR code below:**

Contents

Book 1

The Only LLC Beginner's Guide You'll Ever Need

Limited Liability Companies For Beginners
- Form, Manage & Maintain Your LLC

The Only LLC Beginner's Guide You'll Ever Need

You want to start a business…or even grow your current one to the next level.

Simple enough, right? You find a problem in a market that people need solved… and you solve it. That is the very foundation of any solid business. And the better you are at solving that problem, the more customers you can get!

But what trips many people up is all the legal jargon that comes with starting a business. And that's the situation Jake found himself in. Maybe you can relate.

Jake recently quit his job to start his own business after years of being stuck in a job he hated. He was ready to immerse himself in the design world and enrich people's lives with beautiful graphic designs. He knows a limited liability company ("LLC") will offer him asset protection. However, he's overwhelmed by the complex nature of forming an LLC.

Jake wonders if this is the right move or if he should settle for a sole proprietorship. His business mentor strongly advised him that an LLC was the best move if he wanted to use his money, save on taxes, and protect his assets. As he started the formation process, he hit a roadblock, and now Jake is wondering whether he will succeed in running a business if he cannot figure out how to start an LLC.

As established business owners, we have experienced what Jake is going through. And if you are in the initial stages of starting a business, you could face the same frustrations. For a beginner, LLC formation can seem overwhelming and cause anxiety. You may worry that you are making an expensive legal mistake. The tax rules, business regulations, and legal requirements can make you feel stuck and unable to fulfill your long-awaited dream.

But what if you could simplify the formation process? What if you had a beginner's guidebook that explains the entire process from beginning to end? A book that uses simple English to break down the information you need to successfully establish a legal and functional LLC?

The book in your hands accomplishes this task with precision. "The Only LLC Beginner's Guide You'll Ever Need" promises to show you the right path to take to set up and operate your LLC faultlessly. **Here's some of what you'll learn:**

- The low-down on sole proprietorships, partnerships, corporations, and cooperatives so you can confirm you're making the right move in choosing an LLC.

- Detailed breakdowns of the formation process. Whether choosing a business name or filing documents with the relevant state institutions, we've got you covered.

- A simple explanation of all the legal, business, and financial concepts and requirements so you don't miss any important steps.

- All the documents you need at every stage, ensuring you leave no legal stone unturned.

- Crucial information about taxation, record keeping, operating agreements, and maintaining LLC status.

- Common operational and legal pitfalls that some LLCs grapple with, eventually leading to the loss of their status.

- Advice on expansion and action you must take to open branches in another location or state. We will help you craft a blueprint for growth and build a winning team.

- All the steps to take if a member wants to exit or you decide to sell or close down the LLC.

- Case studies of how business owners succeed in building an empire after following all the information provided in this guide.

You can be sure this information is factual, reliable, and drawn from experience. Under the pen name Garrett Monroe, we are a team of writers in our 40s with varied business experience from multiple industries, including sales, Artificial Intelligence (AI), real estate, business coaching, and accounting. We've brought together our wealth of experience to help you succeed in your business endeavor.

If you want to operate a legitimate business while protecting your assets, this book is for you. Don't struggle in the dark for longer than you should. Interact with the content in this book and let your dreams become a reality. You can form an LLC without stressing out and still preserve a considerable portion of your capital to set up shop. What's the first step for you? Grab a copy of "The Only LLC Beginner's Guide You'll Ever Need" and begin your transformative journey. You'll gain insider strategies and tips it took us years to perfect. This information is now yours for the taking. Flip the pages and start building your business empire the right way.

Chapter 1

Unlocking the LLC: Your Blueprint to Business Freedom

> "Great companies start because the founders want to change the world…not make a fast buck."
> **-Guy Kawasaki**

Starting a business is an adventure that can either be worth the time and effort or leave you feeling drained and with empty pockets. An LLC is a legal structure that enables your entrepreneurial journey to take advantage of key provisions lacking in the other legal structures. As you read this chapter, you will learn what an LLC entails, if it's right for your startup, and the benefits you will enjoy. Before jumping into LLCs, let's explore the other four business structures.

The Fab Four: Business Entities You Need to Know About

As you start your business, the first step is deciding which business structure suits your needs. To ensure you are making the right move in choosing an LLC, we will briefly discuss the four types of business entities under which you can register your business. Being familiar with each entity's main features and tradeoffs will help you pick one that aligns with your circumstances and goals.

Each business structure offers a unique feature that caters to various entrepreneurial needs. Imagine these structures as different pathways leading to the same destination but with varied adventures and challenges along the way. As you read along, have in mind your business identity, financial position, legal footprint, and the people involved.

Sole Proprietorship

A sole proprietorship is the simplest structure to form because you own and run the business as an individual. You have total control of the company and your profits, but you also face unlimited personal liability. When a legal issue arises, or a creditor seeks a pending debt, you may need to pay using your personal possessions.

A sole proprietorship is simple to set up and has minimal paperwork. You only need to obtain permits and licenses that suit your business and location. Fortunately, you do not need to submit formation documents like an LLC or corporation. The simplicity of the starting procedures makes a sole proprietorship a good starting point for new business owners.

New business owners who are aware of the available options shy away from forming a sole proprietorship because they will be responsible for all the management duties and day-to-day work. You also absorb all the risks. Further, your income passes through your personal tax return, and you'll still pay self-employment tax on your business's profit.

If you are starting a simple business with low liability risk, then sole proprietorship is worth considering. But if you plan to take on debt and add employees within a short time, a corporation or LLC may be the better choice.

Partnership

A partnership permits two or more people to share business ownership. As they conduct business, the income and losses flow through to all partners' tax returns. To make it less strenuous to do business together, **the partners draft a partnership agreement outlining:**

- Profit-sharing

- Responsibilities

- Decision-making

- Ownership stakes

Having a written partnership agreement explaining the various roles and powers reduces the number of disagreements when making big or small decisions. Additional guidelines that should be included in the agreement are procedures for adding new partners, buying out partners, and resolving conflicts.

Notably, general partnerships do not require formal registration with your state to function legally. You can formulate your partnership business structure as you see fit. The ease of this setup makes partnership the go-to option for people who need to merge ideas and resources to succeed in starting a business.

Corporation

Corporations have several unique features that make them stand out from the other business structures. The most outstanding one is that it exists as a separate legal entity from the owners and shareholders. This feature protects you from personal liability for the corporation's legal issues and debts that don't go beyond your investment.

Corporations also have ownership shares that you can transfer to interested parties through buying and selling stock. This feature makes it easy to raise capital and allows shareholders to freely trade their shares.

The main disadvantage that corporations face is double taxation. Your business profits are taxed at the corporate and dividend levels. To a greater extent, this feature cancels out the liability protection and fundraising advantage corporations offer.

Another downside to corporations is that they come with more complicated reporting and record-keeping requirements than sole proprietorships, **partnerships, and LLCs. You are required to:**

- Hold shareholder and director meetings.

- Keep accurate corporate minutes.

- File annual reports.

- Comply with the state regulations.

If you are just starting a business, forming a corporation often doesn't make financial and legal sense. But as your company grows and you need to attract outside investment, you may benefit from a corporate structure.

Cooperative

In a cooperative, members come together to form, own, and govern the business. They become equal members in profit sharing and decision-making. The co-op members have equal voting rights in deciding major issues because they collectively own the enterprise.

Its unique feature is that members receive the earnings gained in the form of patronage dividends rather than having shareholders from the general public. In addition, members receive special discounts on services and products.

A cooperative offers new business owners a competitive edge because it empowers them to compete with large competitors by gaining established market share, **which increases their bargaining power. Some drawbacks that may make you shy away from joining a cooperative is the democratic structure that creates challenges such as:**

- Slow decision-making process

- Members prefer short-term over long-term financial benefits

- Reliance on volunteer partnership by members

If you are starting a business in a highly competitive field such as agriculture, utilities, food retailing, healthcare, or financial services, joining a cooperative may be suitable to avoid facing the competition on your own. However, you need to choose one with strong processes because the complex governance structure can slow your growth and limit revenue gains.

There you have it. These are the four business structures you need to know about as we dive into talking about LLCs. Any choice you make from the four structures above or LLC will impact everything, from your financial obligation to personal liability, relationship with partners or shareholders, and capacity for growth.

Is an LLC The Way to Go?

As established business owners from various industries, we can confidently say "Yes," an LLC is the right way to go in many cases. Arguably, an LLC combines the best of both worlds in terms of financial safety. It provides liability protection, has a customizable management structure, offers attractive taxation options, and makes you more credible to potential customers and investors. Let's expand on these game-changing features.

Understanding Liability

No one wants to plan for failure, but the truth is many small businesses and startups don't survive long–term. There are no guarantees of success when starting a business. So, you should protect your personal assets to have your possessions remaining if the business fails. An LLC guarantees that protection as opposed to partnerships or sole proprietorships.

In these structures, creditors can pursue your savings, car, house, or other possessions to get their money back. LLCs successfully prevent this by shielding you from liability. In an LLC, your business exists as a separate entity, and your creditors cannot come after your personal assets if you lose a lawsuit or default on loans.

That said, the liability protection LLCs offer has limitations. For instance, if members do not adhere to all legal formalities or commit fraud, the court overrides this rule and may touch their possessions. In addition, each member directly responsible for injury, harm, or damage remains personally liable for their own negligent actions.

As an illustration, Matt and his four friends established an LLC for outdoor adventures. One summer, Matt leads a hiking tour and fails to secure a client properly, resulting in an injury. In this situation, the LLC shields his friends' personal assets from liability. However, if the court concludes that Matt was grossly negligent and found liable for the injuries, his personal possessions may be used to cover the injury costs.

Management Made Easy

For a startup business, having an outside force like the state dictate how you run and manage your business wouldn't work in your best interest. An LLC provides flexibility in decision-making authority and structuring management, whether you run a manager-managed or member-managed LLC.

In manager-managed LLCs, members appoint qualified managers to oversee day-to-day operations while the rest focus on developing new strategies to grow the business or plan for the future. In member-managed LLCs, all members participate equally in running and managing the business. Decision-making power is often based on majority vote or consensus. This approach keeps all members engaged, but it may also lead to conflict if the guidelines aren't clear.

LLCs also give you more freedom in allocating profit and losses than partnerships. **Members do not have to split everything equally but according to a set of criteria like:**

- Time investment

- Financial contribution

- Sweat equity

- Business generated by each member

Being able to customize your profit sharing and management authority is a benefit you can't afford to overlook. As you create the operating document, ensure you outline everything and treat it as a constitution that guides all aspects of your business.

Pass-through Taxation

Pass-through taxation is one of the primary reasons most entrepreneurs choose LLCs over corporations and it means your profits and losses pass through the business and go directly to individual members. This provision avoids double taxation corporations go through at the corporate and individual dividend levels. This feature minimizes admin work and ensures all members are taxed once, promoting financial efficiency and maximizing your earnings.

LLCs also offer owners the ability to offset business losses against an income earned outside the business on personal tax. For example, if you have a salaried job that gives you $100,000, and your LLC business loses $30,000 in one year - the law allows you to subtract the $30,000 from the wage income on your personal tax return. As a result, the total amount taxable drops from $100,000 to $70,000, leading to considerable tax savings.

As a budding entrepreneur trying to establish yourself, the pass-through taxation allows you to save money and redirect these resources to other areas, such as expanding services or hiring talent.

Credibility & Longevity

When you register a business as an LLC, it becomes a separate legal entity and removes your personal identity from it. As a result, lenders, vendors, and clients may take your business more seriously, knowing you have followed legal procedures permitting you to conduct business.

Registering a business as an LLC makes building business credit in your company's name relatively easy. You can apply for credit, open bank accounts, and establish payment histories on your company's employer identification number (EIN) instead of your social security number—making you more credible.

An LLC structure promotes longevity because the company does not dissolve when a member departs, like in partnerships. Ownership interest can be sold or transferred. Further, creditors cannot force a dissolution through the court even if the business struggles with its resources. This increases the chances of your company's survival past the financial challenges you may face.

LLC Perks: More Than Meets the Eye

While the above advantages based on the business structure are enough to cause you to make a move to form an LLC, the benefits don't stop there. LLCs provide other less obvious perks to make your business grow exponentially. Let's explore them.

Shield Your Personal Wealth

Compared to sole proprietorship and partnership, LLCs protect your personal property, like cars, houses, and investment accounts, from being taken by creditors or other parties that win a financial lawsuit. While this benefit is not absolute, structuring your LLC well will protect your personal wealth far more than other unincorporated entities.

Due to these advantages, entrepreneurs can take more business risks without affecting their family's financial safety. Fortunately, you do not run the risk of filing bankruptcy if all fails, like someone in a partnership or doing business on their own.

Your personal wealth also continues to be protected as your company grows because expanding means you take on more risks. As you add more employees, buy larger equipment, add new locations, or hire more commercial vehicles, your personal possessions still remain shielded from growing liability risks.

Tax Efficiencies

The built-in tax advantages of an LLC ensures the company isn't taxed as an entity, but the members report their share of the profit and losses on their individual return. This provision prevents the company from losing money if they had also been taxed as a business.

In addition, LLCs allow you to choose to be taxed as an S-Corporation or a C-corporation because of the tax election flexibility it offers. The option you choose will help you optimize income and deductions allocations and position you to make strategic income splitting and tax plans. The money you save from these tax-efficient methods can be used to expand the product or service line, drive innovation, or enhance skills development.

Cut the Red Tape - Easy Compliance

An appealing advantage of an LLC compared to a corporation is the ease of compliance. LLCs require less paperwork, minimal administrative duties, and manageable legal regulations. You do not need to issue stock certificates, appoint directors, or hold annual shareholder meetings. In addition, it has fewer accounting formalities than fewer states requiring frequent LLC annual franchise tax payments or annual reporting.

As a start-up, the costs are minimal because you don't have to draft bylaws or issue stock. The legal fees for creating an operating agreement and the filing fees are much less than for corporate formation. If you mainly want to focus on growing your business, an LLC offers the simplicity you need to establish operations.

Gaining the Ability to Raise Capital

LLCs allow you to sell membership interest to investors to fund your startup costs, finance large purchases, or expand operations. You are able to accomplish this without taking on overwhelming debt. You can allow your friends, family members, and outsiders to buy equity stakes in your LLC.

As you add members, you can create various classes of membership having different rights and control the percentage of ownership sold. However, the operating document still governs the profit distribution and rights of new members. The new members still benefit from the pass-through taxation, unlike S Corporations, where the limit is 100 shareholders. This feature enables LLCs to raise significant capital as they retain tax efficiencies and structure flexibility.

The Anatomy of an LLC

LLCs have some crucial components and movable parts that ensure you have meaningful power and flexibility to change things. Being familiar with the primary parts, such as operating agreements, the role of manager and members, and taxation options, helps to demystify LLCs for a beginner. This knowledge ensures your business is positioned for success and adheres to all legal measures. Let's break down the key components to ensure you understand the various parts.

Who's Who: Members & Ownership

Members in an LLC own the company, and membership is not limited to a specific number. Anyone can become a member of an LLC. An individual, partnerships, corporations, trusts, and other LLCs are welcome to join. When these entities join, you create a corporation-like structure with shared risks and investments.

To receive ownership interest, members contribute capital, which is reflected as percentage charges, membership units, or stock analogs. Each member's ownership stake determines their voting rights, profit share, losses, and distribution.

Membership interests can be transferred freely among members or to outsiders. However, they must receive consent from the rest and follow the guidelines in the operating document. You can sell, gift, or pass it on as an inheritance.

Further, LLCs offer reasonable flexibility in structuring ownership, profit-sharing, or investments. Members can also choose to actively manage the LLC or choose managers to oversee day-to-day operations.

Leading the Way: Flexible Management

LLCs offer flexibility in the managerial structure to permit member-managed or manager-managed structures. Small LLCs work well with member-managed structures as they can efficiently perform the day-to-day responsibilities. Decisions require majority approval or a consensus to be accepted and implemented.

Larger LLCs function better by appointing experienced managers to make decisions on behalf of everyone. The manager you hire can be a non-member or a member. Choosing a non-member enables you to hire someone with expertise instead of settling for a member with lower qualifications and experience.

The law also allows LLCs to combine the member and manager-managed structure. For instance, you can hire a general manager to monitor the daily operations but have members retain the authority to make sensitive decisions like large expenditures. The operating agreement acts as a guard to ensure the managerial structure works well by outlining rules regarding electing and removing managers, powers and roles, decision-making processes, and voting procedures. These guidelines prevent confusion and conflicts as the LLC grows.

The Rulebook: Your Operating Agreement

As mentioned above, the LLC operating agreement serves as a governing document and instructional manual for the business [2]. **It goes into detail to explain the following:**

- Voting procedures

- Member rights

- Profit allocations

- Capital contribution

- Manager roles

- Membership transfer

- Dissolution terms

Other details you must include in the document are who can take on debt, enter contracts, sign checks, and purchase assets. Although your state does not require a legal document, having it enables you to align your goals with the rules, provide directions, and avoid conflict between members.

If you do not create this document, the state laws come into effect if you have a dispute and need the court's intervention. The risk you attract in this situation is incomparable to the time and resources you would have used to draft a favorable operating document.

Choose Your Tax Preference

By default, LLCs are taxed as sole proprietorships or partnerships because profits flow through to members' personal tax returns. You can also elect to be a corporation, file with the IRS and choose between an S Corporation (S Corp) or a C Corporation (C Corp).

Choosing S Corp status passes through income and deductions to individual returns while still enjoying corporate benefits. Opting for C Corp means your LLC will incur double taxation but allows your company to retain earnings at lower tax rates and deduct employee benefits.

An LLCs tax planning flexibility can help to simplify the tax planning process. You can adapt as your business grows or faces challenging times. For example, when you begin a business, the profits are crucial for growth, so pass-through taxation is the ideal option. As your business grows, corporate taxation might become appealing as your financial strategies change.

Prestige Points

Doing Business As (DBA) often limits your client, partners, investor, and lender reach. An LLC structure carries more prestige and credibility because it shows you have done your research and are serious about your future business plans.

Customers and lenders feel more comfortable conducting business and signing contracts with an established company than with an unknown

DBA name. Besides, suppliers extend better terms to LLCs over sole proprietorships and partnerships.

Having an LLC next to your company name is like having a badge of honor. When investors or clients see those three letters, they know you are committed to high standards. This impression will increase your trustworthiness—an invaluable quality in the business world. Your LLC will attract more opportunities and grant you access to unimaginable possibilities.

Why Legal Structure Isn't Just Red Tape

As you form the LLC, you may feel like the paperwork is just for legal formalities and doesn't benefit the business to a large extent. However, the content in the paperwork serves additional purposes that go beyond red tape. For instance, the information in the documents protects your assets, boosts credibility, informs your business decisions, and enhances funding potential. It is not about fulfilling an obligation but positioning your company for growth from the first day. Still not convinced? Here are four other reasons why it's more than just formalities.

Dodging Legal Pitfalls

Imagine a situation where a creditor or client sues and wins the lawsuit. If you did not form an LLC and acquired all the paperwork, your personal possessions are at risk of being taken by the plaintiff. The courts can authorize them to access your bank account for the funds, take your house or car, or sell your property or investment to get the money awarded. An LLC enables you to dodge such outcomes because the claims and lawsuits against your business can only affect your company's assets and insurance coverage.

When your business is an LLC, it discourages people from filing superficial lawsuits. Instead, they are likelier to target sole proprietorships with substantial wealth who have not shielded themselves from liability. This benefit doesn't mean you won't face business risks and disputes but that you will be prepared to safeguard your and your family's interests.

The Compliance Code

As you conduct business, you often interact with the term compliance, which mainly targets how you keep your records. Although the rules are less strict than corporations, **you still need to keep records for:**

- Company meetings

- Operational decisions

- Member votes

- Manager appointments

In addition, your business financial records should be completely separate from your personal finances. Have different accounts for business and personal transactions. At the end or beginning of every financial year, ensure you submit annual reports and fees to your state. These compliance requirements prevent occurrences of people taking money from LLCs for personal use. If the state and court find that you have not upheld the various codes, you risk losing your LLC status and incurring additional losses from lawsuits, penalties, or fines.

Deal or No Deal: Business Transactions

Establishing yourself as an LLC attracts more business deals and purchases. Many credible vendors also sell to registered companies because they want the assurance that you have taken the legal measures to do business. Further, lenders approve sizable lines of credit or loans to companies with a functional business structure.

If you plan to make big purchases, doing business without an LLC status may fail to get you the deal. The LLC legal structure offers the seller confidence because it lays out a remedy plan in case of non-payment. Besides, customers and partners prefer getting into contracts with registered companies rather than an individual. LLC gives a sense of safety because you can handle the matter with other members if the original individual leaves the company or disappears.

Magnetize Investors & Partners

The superior quality LLCs offer the original owners is the ability to create shareable equity through membership interests. This feature enables you to attract outside investors more easily than a partnership or sole proprietorship. You can allow investors to buy into your business without the need for strenuous paperwork like that of a corporation.

Co-ownership in an LLC is also more attractive to potential partners because you can run the business with equal rights as a partnership structure but with the LLC benefits. In addition, members can pass their share as inheritance, so investors considering joining don't have to worry about their money being tied up.

Committed and long-term investors often like to join companies that show they have done their homework and planned well. Having the LLC title in your business name makes you a good fit. They also have confidence that your business is there to stay and you are making plans for the future.

As we come to the end of chapter one, you have probably understood that forming an LLC is not only about checking a legal box, but it places you in a strategic position to excel. Although you will put in the work, an LLC is worth the effort as your business grows. In chapter two, we will take you through the planning process and the preparation needed for launching. The information you'll learn will ensure your business starts at an advantageous point and will likely build significant momentum from day one.

The Exact Step-by-Step Guide to Starting Your LLC

Before we get into chapter two, we wanted to quickly lay out the exact LLC set-up process. We'll go more in-depth on these throughout the rest of the book, but this way, you have it here in one place, so you can simply run right through it when setting up your LLC.

Kicking off the process of setting up your LLC is a big deal. It's the first step toward giving your business a solid base. But the admin side of things isn't exactly thrilling for most folks. Still, getting a handle on all the paperwork, legal bits, and financial details is needed.

This next section is about laying down the tracks for your business to run smoothly. So, let's walk through this together, step by step.

Choosing Your LLC's Name & State

Let's talk about picking a name for your LLC. This part's more fun than you might think, but there are a few rules to play by. First up, your LLC's name has to be one of a kind – no stepping on any toes by having a name too similar to another business in your state. And there are a few no-nos to avoid, like using words that might confuse your LLC with a government agency.

So, how do you make sure your LLC's name is ok? Start by brainstorming a list that captures the vibe of your business. Once you've got some contenders, check them against your state's business database – usually something you can do online. Sometimes, you can reserve a name until you're ready to register your LLC officially, which might give you some time while you make a final decision.

Then, as far as choosing a state to incorporate in, here's what you should consider:

- **The location of business operations:** If your business operates in a specific state, it could be beneficial to incorporate there, as it can simplify registration, taxation, and compliance requirements.

- **Taxation:** Different states have different tax structures, including some income taxes, franchise taxes, and sales taxes. Research the tax rates and conditions in different states to determine which is most favorable for your business.

- **Costs and fees:** The fees associated with setting up and maintaining your LLC can vary significantly from state to state. For example, Wyoming, Delaware, New Mexico, Montana, and Colorado have some of the lowest fees.

- **Accessibility to courts:** Does your business anticipate legal disputes? If so, consider the efficiency of the state's court system in handling business-related cases.

- **Legal and regulatory environment:** Each state has its own legal and regulations governing businesses, including employment laws, licensing requirements, and environmental regulations.

Filing the Articles of Organization

Next on the list is tackling the Articles of Organization. Think of this as the official certificate for your LLC. It's where you lay down the basics of your business for the state to see.

First thing's first, you'll need to gather some essential info: the name of your LLC, the address where your business will sit, and the details of your registered agent (that's the person or service authorized to receive legal papers on behalf of your LLC). Some states might ask for a bit more, like the purpose of your business or who's in charge.

Now, onto the common slip-ups. The big one is messing up your registered agent's details. If they're wrong, you might miss important legal notices. Also, double-check that business name to make sure it's exactly the same as the one you reserved. Mismatched names can send your paperwork to rejection.

When your Articles are polished and ready, you'll submit them to the state, usually the Secretary of State's office, and pay a filing fee. This can be done online in most places. And just like that, you're on your way to making your business official. Keep everything accurate, follow the steps, and your LLC will be set up for success.

Appointing a Registered Agent

When choosing a registered agent for your LLC, make sure this person or company is your official go-to for any legal documents. They must be ready and available during business hours to ensure you don't miss anything important.

Here's the deal: you can nominate an individual (yes, even yourself) or go with a professional service. If you're leaning towards an individual, make sure they're reliable and always around to handle documents promptly. On the other hand, a professional service might cost a bit, but they're pros at keeping your paperwork in order and can offer an extra layer of privacy by having their address public, not yours.

The bottom line? Think about your daily schedule and privacy needs. Whether it's you, a buddy, or a service, your registered agent needs to ensure your LLC stays in good standing and legally compliant.

Obtaining an Employer Identification Number (EIN)

Getting your Employer Identification Number (EIN) is next, and it's like having the keys to your new LLC. It's essential for tax filings and opening a bank account for your business. Lucky for you, getting an EIN is easy and free.

Here's how to do it: Head to the IRS website and look for the EIN application page. It's an online form you can breeze through as long as you've got your LLC info ready. You'll fill in details about your LLC, like where it's located and what it does.

The EIN is how the IRS keeps tabs on your business for tax purposes, so it's an important step. Plus, banks usually ask for your EIN when you're setting up a business bank account. It's also handy for hiring employees when you're ready to do so.

You'll get your EIN instantly once you hit submit on the IRS website. Just like that, your LLC is one step closer to being fully operational.

Drafting an Operating Agreement

Even if your LLC is a one-person show, drafting an Operating Agreement is smart. This is the rulebook for how your business runs. It sets clear expectations and helps avoid headaches down the road, especially if you decide to expand or bring on partners.

What goes into this document? Start with your LLC's name, the members, and how you plan to operate. Detail the ownership percentages if you have business partners. Spell out how profits and losses get divvied up.

Also, consider what happens if someone wants out or if you want to add someone to the team. An Operating Agreement covers these scenarios, giving everyone a clear message for handling changes.

This agreement, even for single-member LLCs, means you have a blueprint for operations and a protective shield for your personal assets.

Business Licenses and Permits

Jumping into business means getting comfortable with a few licenses and permits. The requirements can vary depending on what your LLC does and where it's located. For starters, check with your local city or county government to understand the basics. Then, move on to state-level obligations, which might include special permits depending on your industry. Don't forget federal regulations, especially if your business operates in areas like agriculture, alcohol, or aviation. A good tip is to reach out to your local Small Business Administration (SBA) office or a business advisor for a nudge in the right direction. They can help you sift through the maze of regulations.

Setting Up a Business Bank Account

Next up is getting a business bank account, because keeping your personal and business finances separate is important for clarity and legal protection. Choose your bank, and when you're ready, bring your LLC's EIN, Articles of Organization, and Operating Agreement. These documents prove your business's legitimacy and outline who has the authority to manage the funds. A business bank account simplifies tax reporting and bolsters your LLC's credibility with customers and vendors. Plus, it's a solid step toward managing your cash flow.

Compliance and Annual Requirements

Keeping your LLC in good standing involves more than just setting up shop. You'll need to file an annual report with your state every year, which usually involves a fee and a summary of your business's current status. If you use a website like Rocket Lawyer to start your LLC and use their registered agent services, they can handle the annual report filing on your behalf, for an extra fee.

On top of that, staying on top of tax filings, both federally and at the state level, is non-negotiable. Depending on where you're registered, additional compliance tasks or filings might be required. Consider setting reminders or working with a professional to ensure you don't miss any deadlines. Staying diligent with these annual obligations helps avoid penalties and keeps your business on solid legal ground

The Right Websites to Start Your LLC

If you want an easy way to kick off your LLC without having to deal with all the legal requirements yourself, you can look into one of the top websites for starting an LLC. For example:

- **LegalZoom:** They offer LLC formation services along with a wide range of legal documents and services.

- **Rocket Lawyer:** Rocket Lawyer offers comprehensive legal services, including LLC formation, customizable legal documents, registered agents, and attorney consultations.

- **Incfile:** Incfile is known for its affordable pricing and straightforward LLC formation process. They also provide a free registered agent service for the first year.

Key Takeaways

- LLCs are ideal for small businesses because they provide a partnership tax simplicity and corporation liability protection.

- The pass-through taxation element of an LLC enables new business owners to save money by avoiding double taxation.

- Creating a professional operating document with the critical day-to-day issues of operation and authority is vital to prevent disputes and ensure goal achievement.

- The flexible management options LLCs provide allow the members to customize duties and leadership to their advantage.

- LLC business structure gives entrepreneurs more confidence to take more risks because the business structure protects personal assets.

- Business owners must remain compliant with the LLC requirement to continue enjoying the benefits, or else the court or state might override the status.

- The LLC structure gives you a better standing with potential partners, lenders, and customers as it signifies careful planning and professionalism.

- LLCs allow you to form long-term business relationships by offering continuity options such as membership transfer and inheritance.

Chapter 2

Launching Your LLC with Confidence

> "Dream big, start small, but most of all, start.
> -Simon Sinek

Crafting a Business that Resonates

Crafting a business that resonates well with customers is about connecting with them at a personal level. You not only want to provide services or sell products, but you also want to create a lasting bond. Relating with your customers at a personal level is the current trend that new businesses use to win loyalty. In the next section, you will learn how to target your potential customers, choose the right idea, analyze the changing industry patterns, and strategize using the SWOT analysis.

Need-Spotting: Target Market Insights

Understanding your potential customers necessitates knowing your target market and internalizing their needs. **It also requires you to conduct in-depth market research that will help you discover the following:**

- Psychometrics: Your customers' thoughts and emotions influence the goods or services they buy.

- Pain points: What your customer misses that is making them experience pain or difficulty.

- Unmet needs: The desires your potential customers need to be fulfilled.

- Demographics: The people you want to reach, where they live, and what's special about them.

You can implement various methods to conduct an in-depth survey, such as user interviews and online or in-person surveys. Focus groups also work because they help you get the opinion, attitude, and perception of a product or service.

Whichever approach you use, ensure you ask about their frustrations, ideal solutions, challenges, and their typical day surrounding the product or service you want to offer. These questions aim to get an implicit and explicit understanding of their needs.

When gathering the demographic data, go beyond the basic information such as age, gender, and race. Ask about their education level, income, geographical location, religious or spiritual practice, and family size. Anything that will help you focus on the needs related to your service or product. This approach will assist you in learning where existing solutions have failed to address or meet your prospective customers' needs and desires.

Is Your Idea Gold? Evaluating Business Viability

You might be excited that your idea will solve your potential customer's problems. But before running with that idea in your mind, you must evaluate it to determine if it has the potential to foster growth and if it is capable of keeping the momentum long-term. Ask yourself questions such as, how much reach does your idea plan to have? Are the customers you are targeting enough to keep the demand high? Will the idea promote short and long-term growth for your LLC?

A major aspect you need to evaluate is the competition—both direct and indirect competitors. **Questions to have in mind are:**

- How many businesses are already offering relatively the same services or products?

- Have you thought of a way to differentiate your brand from theirs?

- How much are they charging for their services and products?

As you answer these questions, you will be able to tell if you should proceed with your idea or modify it to suit the gaps you discover. Keep in mind - you don't need to reinvent the wheel here. You can build a successful business by mirroring what other successful businesses have already done. After all, they've proven there's a market for it. Just make sure to put your own spin on it.

Next, you must assess your readiness to meet the regulatory and financial requirements to start your business. Do you have enough money to actualize your idea? Will you have difficulty getting certified or acquiring the necessary licenses and permits? Do you need partners or co-founders to help you add the qualifications and skills you need to form and operate a business?

Additionally, consider your strengths and weaknesses and your passion for business. Will you persevere through the entire process of opening and running a business? Take the time to reflect and honestly answer this question.

Analyzing Industry Trends and Shifts

Staying ahead in your industry is all about learning and tracing the changes occurring in the market and adjusting your business plan. As you keep track of shifting trends, you'll spot threats and notice emerging opportunities. **Some factors affecting industry changes include the following:**

- Evolving cultural trends that impact the attitudes of your customers. Investigate what caused the shift and make changes where necessary.

- The current movement of people in your business's locality. Are more people moving in or out of your area? If you're losing customers due to a decline in your target market, research new ways to remain relevant.

- Pay close attention to the target demographic in your area. Changes can impact the future of your business. Once you identify these trends, plan accordingly.

- One age group is moving to another stage in life. Your product or service may lose relevance if you do not adjust or modify the product. For example, baby boomers are retiring, and Gen Zers are getting married or having children.

- Understand the technological changes affecting businesses, especially the emergence of AI. Some entrepreneurs are losing revenue, while others are celebrating the creation of new business opportunities.

After studying the above changes, adjust your services and products to meet the current demand and remain relevant.

SWOT: The Full Picture

SWOT analysis helps you get a holistic picture of how your business will perform in relation to particular internal and external factors. The internal factors focus on your strengths and weaknesses, while the external factors assess the opportunities and threats in your business environment. Creating a strategic plan around these four elements will help you base your company's decisions on facts. The following table summarizes the areas each letter in SWOT evaluates and the examples involved.

SWOT Analysis	Evaluates	Examples
Strengths	Advantages you have that make your business stand out	- Skilled team members - High capital - Unique brand - Low debt - Tax advantages
Weaknesses	Aspects that put your business at risk of performing poorly	- High costs - Poor market research done - Fewer assets - Lack of specialized skills - Poor credit score
Opportunities	External factors to take advantage of to grow your business	- Partnerships - Increasing population

		- Better technology advances - Less stringent regulatory demands
Threats	Outside forces that can hinder your business from thriving	-New advanced products - Dishonest competition -Negative economic shift -Unfavorable regulations

SWOT analysis is a comprehensive model that requires a team to help you analyze everything objectively and with precision. Recruit partners, LLC members, trusted customers, and professionals to help you succeed in coming up with a practical SWOT report.

Afterward, address those factors that are significant or present the greatest risk of losing revenue. For example, if one of your weaknesses is a lack of specialized skill, you can employ someone to fill that role or investigate how technology (as an emerging opportunity) can cover that weakness.

Dive Before You Launch

It is exciting to see your dream becoming a reality. Launching a business is a big step you are about to undertake, but you first need to do your homework. Diving before you launch necessitates thoroughly researching the market to ensure you target the right people. It also requires you to study your competition and set the right price. Let's expound more on these points.

Segmentation: Who's Your Crowd?

Finding your crowd entails knowing who you are targeting with your product. It's about narrowing down the specific people who will need or want to buy what you are offering [3]. Are you planning to sell your product or services to 40-year-olds or 20-year-olds or a mixed-age group? Which income bracket are they in? What lifestyle habits do they have? These questions will inform how you package and advertise your services or products.

For most businesses, their product or service does not meet everyone's needs. Your business is going to solve a problem or satisfy a need for a segment of the market. For example, a business owner may have formulated a new hair product similar to those in the market but has a unique quality because it is organic and environmentally friendly. This entrepreneur will ensure the packaging style is environmentally conscious and leans towards a minimalist design.

To choose the most favorable crowd, you must conduct thorough research in the locality you want to set up shop. Afterward, you will direct your resources and use your energy to satisfy the needs of the segment that most suit your product or service. Expanding your reach by watering down your offering may cause you to lose revenue. At the beginning, choose one segment and take a risk with them. As your business grows, you can add another segment as you open new locations or add more departments.

Friends & Foes: The Competitive Landscape

Before launching your business, you must analyze your competitive landscape by studying the existing companies. Your aim is to learn how they conduct their business. **Examples of crucial areas to focus on include:**

- Products and services

- Packaging methods

- Marketing strategies

- Online presence

- Unique selling point

The information you collect as you assess the above variables will help to reveal the gaps present, and hopefully, you can fill them. In your data collection process, you will notice two types of competitors: direct and indirect. For instance, if you plan to establish a vegetarian restaurant, your direct competitors would be the other vegetarian stores. In contrast, your indirect competitors would include the retail shop selling raw veggies. In formulating your business strategy, identify the measures you will take to tackle the two groups of competitors.

Finally, find out the potential barriers to opening a business in that area. Will the competitors fight you? What plans are in place to mitigate risks associated with rival companies? How you address this situation depends on whether you'll have an e-commerce store or only a retail shop.

Reading Minds: Deciphering Customer Behavior

Knowing your customers' behavior entails understanding what they like and dislike, how they buy, and why they prefer particular products over others in the market. These findings will help you in assessing how your prospective consumers purchase things. Today's marketing approach is not about who will buy what you are selling but how and why your potential customers are shopping for that particular product or service.

Ask yourself, how frequently do the people you are targeting shop? Why do certain products sell better than others? How effective is your marketing? Businesses learn a lot by paying attention to three key variables they use in understanding consumer behavior. **These are:**

- **Personality traits:** Are these customers extroverts or introverted? What is their background? How were they brought up?

- **Social traits:** Are your potential customers susceptible to external factors like advertisements, peers, and news?

- **Psychological responses:** How do customers feel about your services or products? Are their reactions based on their personality traits, or are they situational? What steps can your business take to improve how customers feel about your services? Answering these questions can give you key insights into ways to adapt strategies to improve.

Understanding the above factors is crucial to establishing a solid foundation for your business. Discover what makes them happy, sad, or angry. Use such knowledge to solve their problems.

Pricing Mastery: Setting it Right

Setting the price right requires you to gather information on how your competitors have priced their product or service, your cost of production, the discount you want to offer as a start-up, and your desired profit margins. You will use one or a combination of these factors to set your price. **The following are examples of variations for setting the price:**

- Set your price above the cost of production but at a cost your customers are willing to pay (value-based pricing).

- Focus on your profit margins so you factor in the cost of production and the profit you plan to make (cost-plus pricing).

- Work with your competitor's prices and charge the same price, slightly below or above their price (competitive pricing).

- Focus on getting into the market and attracting customers using a price that is not your ideal but will increase after you get loyal customers (penetration pricing).

- Set the price as per your customers' location (geographical pricing).

- Set the price in relation to a customer's emotions or subconscious mindset. For example, setting the price at $19.99 instead of $20 (psychological pricing).

Realistically, if you sell numerous products or services, you will eventually use a customized combination of the above pricing strategies. As you come up with the price, monitor your customers' responses and adjust accordingly. Ensure your marketing strategy includes an in-depth explanation of the value your product or service provides—you want your customer to feel they got value for their money.

Naming Your LLC: More than Just Words

Naming your LLC is an important decision you should make with exceptional care. It has to be a unique name, though it should let your prospective customers know which brand of products and services you offer. There are laws and regulations applicable to your state and industry, which we'll discuss in more detail below. This section discusses more about the factors you should bear in mind while naming your LLC.

Branding: Beyond the Logo

Branding your LLC is more than just creating an engaging logo. Indeed, the logo must convey to your customers exactly what your business stands for and reveal your personality. But branding goes beyond that. Branding is the essence of your reputation and how you want your LLC to be viewed. Branding also affects how your customers feel and think when interacting with your company.

As you develop your brand, find a professional or trusted partner who can help you analyze what you have in store for your customers and how it is better and different from what the competitors have been offering them.

Defining your mission is the first step in developing a unique brand. This step entails identifying why you are going into business, what motivates you, and the values you want the customers to experience. Reflecting on these issues will help to clarify why you're becoming an entrepreneur and provide you with an accurate mission statement.

Choosing the right brand also means figuring out what makes you and your business unique. You are selling your story, personality, character, background, and other unique factors. So, consider what makes your offering different from that of other sellers in the market.

Digital Real Estate: Domain Checks

After choosing a suitable name for your business, you need to check online whether the name is already registered. Sometimes, people in digital real estate register various domain names and then sell them to entrepreneurs. Domain pricing depends on how hard they worked to get a noticeable presence online.

Follow these steps to check the availability of the domain you have in mind if buying an existing digital domain is not part of your plan:

- Visit any domain registrar such as GoDaddy, Namecheap, or Bluehost and search for your business name. If the name is already taken, these platforms will help generate suggestions specific to your business name.

- Use a domain search tool that is dedicated to that purpose. Examples include DomainWheel, Business Name Generator, and Domains Bot. These tools will confirm if the name is available or suggest names you can use once you enter your business name.

- Perform a simple web search by typing in the domain name you want to use and clicking search. If a website is already online, you must abandon that domain name and look for variations. If the search results show "this site can't be reached," you probably have a domain name. But you should cross-check several times to ensure it wasn't an internet or website glitch.

Once you find an available domain, quickly reserve it because someone else could have the same idea.

Legally Yours: Trademark Navigations

A trademark is another way to distinguish yourself from your competitors and for customers to recognize you. Its main function is to legally protect your brand, assist you in safeguarding your product or service against fraud or counterfeiting, and identify the source of your service and goods.

You can register your trademark with the state authority in charge of the trademark or with the United States Patent and Trademark Office (USPTO). State registration is easier and less expensive than federal registration. However, it limits your reach. Once you go online, you have a more national and international reach that may pose a challenge to trademark ownership.

Similar to domain checks, you need to conduct an online search before filing an application to register your company's trademark. Searching will avoid closely-related duplication, and the filing fee is non-refundable once USPTO rejects your application due to unavailability. If possible, it is better to trademark your LLC at the beginning rather than using the name, and after building a solid brand, you realize you have to change it because it's in existence.

Stickiness: Crafting Memorable Names

If you want to enhance your brand engagement and have a lasting impact, especially for first-time customers, you must have a memorable name that sticks with your clients. A sticky name grabs the customers' attention, establishes a connection, and leaves a lasting impression.

To choose a memorable business name, make sure it evokes emotions. Examples include joy, empathy, trust, intrigue, and curiosity. Also, pick a simple name that still states what you are all about. Short and easy-to-pronounce names are memorable. However, a long and complicated name will confuse people and may even scare away potential clients.

Further, it is important to use known terms, expressions, and signs while naming a product or company. People tend to relate more to what they know, and they go for concepts that are recognizable rather than unpacking new ones. Secondly, you will command greater confidence and trust within a short time.

Legal Foundations: Beyond the Basics

After internalizing the basic requirements for starting a business discussed so far, it is time to go deeper by looking at the legal side of things. At the onset, it may sound like a complex process, but we endeavor to simplify the content to help you understand. We will discuss the regulations and compliance needs, the permits and licenses you must acquire, and how your business location matters.

Rules of the Land: Navigating Regulations

Every business must follow the rules of the land, which are created by the local authorities, state officials, and the federal government. Take time to study the regulations at each level and categorize them according to must-haves and those good to have. A key responsibility that comes with the LLC name is ensuring you abide by the regulations at all levels.

Without a doubt, keeping up with the regulations can be overwhelming and act as an obstacle for you to get started. However, you must take the bull by the horns and address them to ensure you stay in business. **To get started, here are some ways to navigate the regulatory process:**

- Learn about the regulations and update your information through ongoing research, subscribing to reliable industry newsletters, and visiting the regulatory websites monthly or quarterly.

- Form a team of trusted individuals who can help you create a system geared towards staying compliant. They can help you develop the policies, procedures, and protocols needed to ease adherence monitoring.

- Embrace technology and use it to streamline tasks, documents, and activities to ensure they meet local, state, and federal regulatory standards.

- Ask for guidance from experts in various fields related to regulatory requirements. For example, consult a corporate lawyer to help ensure your documents meet the standards or talk to an accountant to confirm your records have all the required information.

As you interact with the various regulatory stakeholders, make it your mission to form a working relationship beyond inspection. Seek to win them over to your side and show them your intention of creating value for everyone's benefit, including them.

Staying Compliant in Your Industry

Once you know the regulations specific to your business, you must prioritize staying compliant. A foundational step is complying with the LLC business structure, such as creating the proper documents, meeting the membership requirements, holding the required meetings, and sending reports before deadlines

After meeting the general compliance requirements, you should focus on the more specific requirements for your business. For example, if you are opening a business that requires storing people's sensitive information, you must know the US data privacy protection laws that mandate you to protect your customers' information. **Staying compliant attracts the following benefits:**

- Covers your business against legal actions that could have been avoided. Non-compliance opens a loophole that customers, other companies, or authorities can exploit. You may end up paying huge settlement fees that are incomparable with the cost you would have incurred staying compliant.

- Safeguards your business from losing customers because they cannot trust your product or services after you violate a law. For example, if you own a restaurant and authorities discover that your employees do not receive any training in food handling.

- Saves you money by avoiding huge fines for ignoring compliance regulations. Your business license may be revoked or suspended for an extended period.

- Ensures business continuity when you maintain compliance. For instance, if you miss one crucial LLC requirement, you risk losing the name and the benefits that ensure long-term success.

It is important to note that business laws and regulations do not remain constant. They keep changing, and this requires you to stay vigilant.

Compliance is an ongoing process. Make it your goal to stay current with the external and internal business compliance requirements.

An Updated Reporting Requirement for 2024 and Beyond

Starting in 2024, LLCs and Corporations must file a Beneficial Owner Information Report (BOI). Reports started being accepted in January of 2024, and if you registered your LLC prior to January 1, 2024, you will have until January 1, 2025, to report the BOI. If your company registered on or after January 1, 2024, you will have 30 days of notice of creation or registration.

You can learn more and file your report here:

https://www.fincen.gov/boi

Getting the Green Light: Licenses & Permits

Acquiring licenses and permits is a crucial step that gives you the green light to open your doors for business. Licenses and permits have a general purpose, although their definitions differ. A license grants an individual or business permission to do something. It is used to guarantee competence in what you want to do.

Permits, on the other hand, monitor safety issues and seek to ensure you prioritize the customer's well-being. For example, you need a health permit to open a restaurant or clinic. These licenses and permits are issued by the federal, state, county, municipal, and city governments.

The following table gives examples of licenses and permits you may need to operate a business.

License and permit requirements	Concerned institution	Examples of business
Starting a business	Federal and state	Any venture that will sell products or offer services
Business activities regulated nationally	Federal government	Alcohol, agriculture, and food preparation
Legal structure	State government	Corporations, NGOs, LLCs, or partnerships
Employment Identification Number	Federal government	Any business with employees
Zoning permit	Local government	Operate a business in a particular location
Health permit	County health department	Handle food or in contact with the human body
Sales tax license	State government	Sell goods or services

Location Matters: Zoning Know-hows

When contemplating a business location, you need to look for things like zoning laws, how much in tax you will be paying, customers' proximity, and the regulatory requirements of operating within that area. The choice of location must also take into consideration the nature of the product or service that you sell. In addition, keep in mind the expenses that will go into choosing a specific location. **Factors to consider that change according to location include:**

- Rental rates

- Utilities

- Property value

- Business insurance rate

- Minimum wages

- Government fees and licenses

When searching for a rental space for your business, look into the area's zoning laws. For instance, some local authorities prohibit business owners from operating their businesses within residential or restricted zones. Additionally, the zone you choose should match your budget and meet your business standards. For example, if you intend to provide premium services, a luxurious and quiet site would work better than a strip mall-type location in a noisy area.

Another factor to consider in zoning matters is the tax landscape. Sales tax, income tax, corporate tax, and property tax differ from place to place. Look for a state or county that creates a tax-friendly environment for certain companies. Besides, some states or local governments also give special tax credits, favorable loans, and other financial incentives to support new businesses. So, think through these factors before you settle on a location.

Blueprint of a Bulletproof Business Plan

Starting a business without knowing exactly what you will be offering customers or how you will execute various roles and responsibilities is a recipe for disaster. Your business may grow fast, but you lack a plan to take advantage of this opportunity and lose customers or experience burnout.

Conversely, your business may lag, and you lose revenue because you have no reference point on what action to take. A bulletproof business plan takes care of either outcome. It helps you have a contingency plan and know how to respond to emerging challenges. What should you include in a business plan? Let's answer that question for you.

Purpose-Driven: Crafting Mission & Vision

Crafting a mission or vision statement requires deep thought. It should capture what your business will be about and also tell your customers where you want to go. Even though you aren't fully clear on the direction you want your business to take in the future, make sure the mission and vision statements capture your values.

Ideally, you should create your vision statement first because it carries the overall big idea. Afterward, craft your mission statement, which involves developing a practical and step-focused statement that informs the LLC members and the public how you plan to achieve the vision. **Questions you should ask yourself as you draft your vision are:**

- What purpose do I want my vision to serve?

- Why do I want my business to exist?

- What core values do I want to have for my business?

- What would my customers miss if my business closed down?

As you create your vision, make it relatable and let people feel they are not only buying a product or using your services but also joining a movement or culture that inspires them. A vision statement often remains the same for an extended period, but the mission statement may change as your business grows and you become clear on what you want to focus on.

Captivating Customers: Sales & Marketing Mastery

As you start your business, you want to find ways of attracting potential customers to purchase your services or products. At this stage, you must understand your target customers and design your sales and marketing strategies with that in mind. For example, college students prefer colorful, modern advertising styles that appeal to their emotions. People in their 40s and above prefer an advertisement focusing on how the product will work for them rather than how it will make them feel.

Mastering sales and marketing strategy means creating an experience that will captivate your customers until they become loyal to you. It also involves maintaining or improving the standards you set from the beginning. Compromising your products or services to make more revenue after you get customers is likely to affect sales in the long run. **Examples of marketing activities include:**

- Relationship building

- Having a social media presence

- Advertising

- Merchandising

- Publicity

Captivating your customers is an ongoing task. You must be willing to

change your strategies as you study the market and your customer's behavior. Aim to impress them by satisfying their needs and wants as you also acquire and attract new customers with your unique selling point.

Numbers Don't Lie: Budgets & Projections

The most important aspect that will help to tell if your business is making profits or losses is a well-crafted budget. Keeping an updated and factual budget will help you increase opportunities for investors and loans while reducing your need to acquire debt.

Making projections is also made possible when you keep an accurate budget. It enables you to review your previous data and project the revenue you might make in the next few months. Although, you may need to adjust your projections as the economy or landscape changes.

The main components of a basic business budget are the sales and revenue, total costs and expenses, and the profit or loss section. However, to make projections, **you need three crucial reports that you should keep.**

- **Cash flow statement:** Monitors how things flow in and out of the business. It includes cash and non-cash items.

- **Income statement:** Gives an overview of a business's net income, expenses, and revenue.

- **Balance sheet:** General picture of your company's assets and liabilities

Keeping accurate records is a key marker of how your business performs. Even when you are faring well by the number of customers you have, it is the final tally in your budget that tells you if these customers have helped you reach your financial goal. Numbers don't lie, so be vigilant about keeping accurate financial records.

Setting the Bar: Milestones & KPIs

Setting the bar high for your business requires you to track whether it is achieving its goals or not. Although there are several ways of monitoring progress, Key Performance Indicators (KPIs) and Milestones are the most commonly used, especially for new and emerging businesses.

KPI measures how well your business achieves its goals in various departments. For example, the marketing team will monitor their performance by the number of new customers or people reached by their strategies. The sales team will measure their performance by comparing data on previous and current sales records. KPI helps track if you are meeting your objectives and lets you see potential risks and new opportunities.

Milestones are used to measure one major event as opposed to KPIs that monitor ongoing progress. Milestones bring together the KPIs at the end of a certain period and assist you in checking if you are closer to achieving your big goal. For example, you may have a milestone of winning 100 loyal customers in the first three months.

KPI keeps track of what you are doing to achieve this goal, while the milestone confirms if you will accomplish this goal in three months. Established companies use milestones to reward employees and celebrate achievements as a way to motivate everyone to keep putting more effort into achieving the business goals.

Key Takeaways

- Analyzing industry shifts entails keeping up with the trends and changes that take place in your area of business.

- Thoroughly researching the market is a critical task to ensure you target the right people. You must also narrow down to the specific people who will need or want to buy what you are offering.

- Branding determines how people feel, think, and say about your business. Think deeply about your values, your reason for starting the business, and your unique selling points.

- Checking for digital presence is part of a name search. Choose a business name that also has a domain name available.

- Take time to study the regulations and compliance requirements at each level and categorize them according to must-haves and those good to have.

- The location you choose for your business must suit the product and service you want to offer. It should also limit your expenses and increase your customer reach.

- Create a vision and mission statement that is relatable and makes people feel they are not only buying a product or using your services but also joining a movement or culture that inspires them.

- Mastering sales and marketing strategy means creating an experience that will captivate your customers until they become loyal to you.

By the way, if you'd like to see the best websites to instantly launch your LLC, you can download here as part of our free 7-Figure Business Toolkit: llclegend.com/llc-s-corp-bonus

Chapter 3

Mastering Your LLC Formation

"If you don't build your dream, someone else will hire you to help
them build theirs.
-Dhirubhai Ambani

Picking the Perfect State for Registration

The state you choose to register your LLC will determine your
company's viability and success. It is the place you'll house your business
and generate revenue. Let's consider other important factors as you
settle down on the location.

Weighing the State Factors: Tax, Rules, and Anonymity

Taxes, rules, and anonymity are three factors that most entrepreneurs
consider before choosing the state to register their LLC. For instance,
corporate taxes differ by state because of the different deductions and
exclusions. For example, Alabama's corporate tax is 6.5%, Colorado's is
4.5%, and Massachusetts's is 8%.

**Every state also has its own rules and regulations for LLCs.
Variation occurs in the finer details, such as:**

- The amount required as capital

- How often the reporting should be done

- The laws and regulations governing the formation and operation

- Who can be your registered agent

Some states, such as Wyoming, Delaware, Nevada, and New Mexico, don't reveal the details of the manager, members, and even owners. Other states have this provision but with limitations.

Why Everyone Talks About Delaware (And Other Options)

Did you know that more than half of Fortune 500 companies are incorporated in Delaware? They chose this state because Delaware offers significant flexibility and advantages for LLCs. For example, Delaware's privacy laws are stronger, meaning you are not required to reveal too many details about your LLC. In addition, Delaware offers attractive tax benefits; for example, the state doesn't require you to pay income tax if your business is in another state.

Nevada, Wyoming, New Mexico, Iowa, North Dakota, and Tennessee are other states to consider forming an LLC. Each state has one or more benefits that make it stand out. For example, Wyoming and Kentucky are among the cheapest states to form an LLC, while Nevada has favorable features for a single-member LLC.

Going Big: Multi-State Operations and Foreign Qualifications

As your business grows, you may consider extending to other states outside the state where you registered your LLC. The process to make this request is called foreign qualification or state registration. The language can seem confusing, but "foreign" refers to any state outside the one where the LLC is initially registered [5]. Once you qualify, you'll receive authority to conduct business in another state as a qualified foreign company.

The procedure follows the same criteria as the initial formation. You need to fill out documents containing information about your company, referred to as an Application for a Certificate of Authority or Application of Registration. Most states require a Certificate of Good Standing or a Certificate of Existence.

The Right Hand of Your LLC: The Registered Agent

A registered agent is an important person in your LLC, and you must choose them carefully. It is a legal requirement to have a registered agent for your LLC in all states. Let's break down their duties, how to pick one, and what to do when you need to update their details.

Decoding the Role of a Registered Agent

A registered agent is considered by your state as the only legal way for the courts, government, and the public to contact your company. Your registered agent's information is usually in the public domain, and anyone can access their contact when they search online or in person. **You need a registered agent to fulfill the following functions:**

- Provide an official point where the government can contact you regarding compliance or tax matters.

- Receive legal documents from individuals or entities for or against your company.

- Receive notification of important changes at the federal, state, or local level.

As they carry out these roles, you can stay on top of issues because that makes you aware of important deadlines and actions you must address.

Picking the Perfect Agent: What to Look For

If you mainly operate online or have a mobile office, you must take all the measures to ensure you pick the perfect agent. So, what do you look for in a registered agent? Let's explain using a table.

Qualification of an Agent	Reason
Expertise	Must know about LLCs and understand the compliance rules
Availability	Must be reachable every day and during working hours to deliver all documents
Efficient services	Must have technological means and physical capabilities to offer superior services
Wide reach	Must be able to deliver any information or documentation anywhere in the state of your business and beyond

A registered agent should be more than just a person who delivers documents. They should be someone who can also advise you regarding LLC matters and how to respond to some complex information.

Expert Agent or Do-It-Yourself? Making the Choice

The law allows you to list yourself as the registered agent for your company. You can consider becoming your own agent if you want to cut costs and don't plan on moving around regularly. In addition, if you can keep track of all communications, documents, and deadlines and are highly organized to get it done, then being your own agent is a viable option.

Being your own agent also comes with some disadvantages you must consider. For instance, if you are sensitive about security matters, having your personal details like name and physical address in the public domain will not sit well with you. Besides, being an agent also restricts your movement and makes it impossible for you to receive all the documentation if you have multiple locations.

When and How to Update Your Agent Details

Sometimes, you may wish to hire a different registered agent, or your current agent may inform you their contact information has changed. The law requires you to immediately update the contact information via your state's business filing agency. The procedure is simple. You download the form online, fill and upload or email it. Some states require you to mail it.

If you fail to update the information, you will be fined. Your Certificate of Good Standing may also be revoked, or your company dissolved if the state discovers you operated without a valid agent for a prolonged period.

Crafting a Solid Foundation: The Articles of Organization

The Articles of Organization are the documents you need to establish an LLC with the state. It is used to recognize you as a legal entity promising to conduct business by the state laws. All the benefits of an LLC become realized after filing this document and receiving approval from the state.

The Essentials for Your Articles

Every state has different requirements for the Articles of Organization. Some ask for detailed information, while others require basic information only. **The general information you'll be asked for in any state is as follows:**

- Your LLC's name

- The physical address of the main place of business

- Your agent's name and mailing address

- Effective date of starting operations

The additional information you may need to submit includes detailed information about your members and manager, why you are forming the LLC, and the duration of the company. Most states will require you to provide an annual report with a small fee charged, while others expect you to submit a brief report at no charge.

Navigating the Filing Labyrinth: Fees and Steps

Once you know the requirements needed in the Articles of Organization, the next step is getting it done. You must file the documents with your state's business filing agency under the Secretary of State. **The following are the steps you will take:**

1. Access the filing document in your state's online platform or enter their offices to acquire a copy.

2. Fill out the articles of organization accurately and file them as advised.

3. Pay the filing and formation fee.

4. Receive the certificate of formation via mail or email.

5. If need be, publish a notice of formation.

Filing fees range from state to state. It can be as high as $275 (Massachusetts) or as low as $40 (Kentucky). Some states, like South Carolina, Mississippi, Missouri, and Arizona, do not charge annual filing fees, while others charge a fee ranging from $7 to $300.

Note: if you use a site like RocketLawyer.com to set up your LLC, they can do the filing for you for a small fee.

Digital vs Snail Mail: Which Route to Choose?

Articles of Organization are crucial documents. You want to choose the best method to file, receive, and store them. Snail mail could be the option most favorable for you because it's more reliable when stored well and gives you a personal touch. Digital filing is cheaper, faster to access and send, and easy to trace. Whichever option you pick, consider the time taken to exchange documents, cost, and security level.

Adapting and Updating: Tweaking the Articles

You rarely need to amend the Articles of Organization if you get it right the first time. However, you may get to a point where you need to change the LLC's name or physical address, financial structure, management, membership, and the registered agent. Once you determine what you need to change, your next step will be to obtain approval from the members, fill out the specific form for changing the document, file the new document with the agency, pay the fees, receive approval, and adjust your company's document.

Drafting the Operating Blueprint: The Easy Guide

Only five states require that you file your operating document. These are:

1. New York

2. Maine

3. Delaware

4. Missouri

5. California

As business owners, we recommend you create one to ensure your company functions optimally and with minimal disputes. Let's have a closer look at this crucial document.

Why Your LLC Can't Go Without an Operating Agreement

Not having an Operating Agreement means the state laws will govern how you conduct your company operations. For example, most state laws stipulate that profit should be divided equally among members. If this is not the plan you had in mind, some members may bear a heavier burden if the capital contribution differs significantly. Also, the operating agreement will minimize and eliminate disputes arising not only about money but also about authority, duties, and record-keeping.

Customize the Agreement

Customization to best suit your business objectives involves creating an operating agreement that clearly stipulates your goals and objectives. It means leaving nothing to chance but outlining all the rules, rights, and duties of the owners, individual members, managers, and the entire group. An operating document allows you to completely separate your personal affairs and business matters to the level that suits you but is done for the greater good of the company.

Delineating the Power: Roles, Rights, and Duties

The operating document you create depends on whether your company is a single or multi-member LLC. A single-member LLC makes it easier to formulate an operating document because you have all the voting rights and a 100% ownership percentage. **For the multi-member LLC, the operating agreement must break down issues such as:**

- What each member contributed as capital and the rights they receive

- The roles of each member and which criteria will be used to assign duties

- The voting rights of each member and the weight it carries

- Who has the right and power to make crucial decisions

Keeping the Blueprint Fresh: Revisions and Overhauls

Since you and your members created the operating document, you can make changes anytime your company grows, experiences challenges, or evolves. The amendments you make should still reflect your desires, include updated information, and consider the current market needs. To avoid disputes, your initial operating agreement should include a section on how you'll implement the amendment. Do members need to vote for it to be amended, or can the owner decide if and when it should be amended?

Unlocking Business Power with Your EIN

An Employment Identification Number (EIN) is a nine-digit figure the IRS uses to identify taxpayers. Getting the EIN doesn't depend on whether you have employees; every business owner should have one.

Why Every LLC Needs its EIN Badge

An EIN badge is a crucial requirement to operate a business in America. This number enables businesses to file and pay federal tax returns. Besides, you cannot open a business bank account without an EIN. The bank requires your EIN to identify and link your company to your account. Further, the law does not permit you to have employees without an EIN, and you may not receive some business permit or license without producing your EIN.

EIN 101: The Quick Guide to IRS Application

For the reasons stated above, it is impossible to run your business without an EIN. **Here is a quick and easy guide to applying and acquiring your LLC:**

1. Visit the IRS website [6] and navigate to apply for EIN (under file, then popular navigation bar)

2. You will be required to give your taxpayer identification number

3. Fill out the form in one session (you cannot save it to complete later)

4. Submit the form, and you'll receive your EIN immediately.

5. Download or print your EIN notice for reference or use

Beyond Identification: The EIN's Extended Role

As mentioned, EIN has more roles than just giving your business an identity with federal and state institutions. It also enables you to keep separate records of your personal assets and your matters. This provision ensures you protect your personal possessions from liability. As your company grows, an EIN also facilitates the investment of surplus cash. You can use the EIN to open a brokerage account and buy stocks.

Stay Current: Managing EIN Alterations and Shifts

The EIN rarely changes and will be associated with your company unless a   significant change occurs. Examples of changes include moving from a single-member LLC to a multi-member LLC or a single-member LLC wanting to be taxed as S-Corp. If you received an EIN and wish not to use it, you can request the IRS to close the business account. The IRS will suspend the account without penalty, but the EIN will remain.

Key Takeaways

- The state you choose to host your company will determine your taxes, the extent of rules you'll follow, and how anonymous you will be to the general public.

- A registered agent should be more than just someone who receives and delivers documents; they should also advise you regarding LLC matters.

- You enjoy all the benefits of an LLC after filing your articles of organization and receiving approval from the state.

- Failing to draft an operating agreement for your business means that state laws will govern how you conduct your company's operations.

- Create an operating agreement that clearly stipulates your goals and objectives, leaving nothing to chance but outlining all the rules, rights, and duties of the owners, individual members, managers, and the entire group.

- An EIN enables companies to pay taxes, open bank accounts, apply for loans, and receive business permits and licenses.

Chapter 4

Mastering LLC Management

Unlocking the Power of Member Roles and Responsibilities

Members are individuals or entities with a membership interest in your LLC. These individuals can make or break your business, and care needs to be taken about how you handle them. This section will explore the various roles and responsibilities of an LLC member.

Defining Member Duties: Who Does What?

The duties of members in an LLC depend on whether you choose to have it as a member-managed or manager-managed LLC. In a member-managed LLC, the members take full responsibility for the day-to-day running of the business and make crucial decisions. In a manager-managed LLC, the members actively choose a manager to perform the daily errands but only participate in major decision-making. **Generally, the roles of members in an LLC are:**

- Creating and maintaining LLC documents

- Ensuring personal and business finances remain separate

- Entering and signing contracts with vendors and lenders

- Acquiring licenses and filing annual reports

- Voting on diverse issues

The duties each member receives depend on the consensus reached in meetings and what is outlined in the operating agreement.

Voting Rights: Making Decisions That Matter

All members of an LLC have the right to vote. The issue at hand and the weight of their vote differs. The manager-managed structure limits the voting power of members. The members often elect managers, and they make the day-to-day decisions. Members come in to vote on major issues, such as adding new members, contemplating dissolution or merger, and amendment of various documents. The member manager structure gives members the right to vote on all matters concerning the business.

Managing Conflicts: The Art of Resolution

Conflicts among members can arise due to the failure of some members to perform or complete tasks, disagreement on leadership methods, work ethic, and personality differences. While all conflicts need to be addressed, some conflicts are too severe and can affect the running of the business [7]. **Here are ways to resolve an arising conflict:**

1. Have a clear outline of how to address various conflicts in the operating agreement and refer to it.

2. Approach conflict as an opportunity for growth and model that to the members.

3. If possible, involve everyone in developing the resolution formula.

4. Train and model ways to resolve conflict amongst members, such as healthy accommodation, collaboration, and compromise.

Never allow conflict to drag on for days or weeks. Instead, have a system in place that identifies emerging conflict and takes concrete predetermined steps to address issues before they become major issues.

Membership Changes: Adding and Removing Members

Adding or removing members is a major change in an LLC that requires you to amend your formation documents. In most situations, you must inform the IRS and other major institutions of the change. Changing members could mean adjusting your ownership percentage or selling the entire business. The operating document and Articles of Organization should have this provision—allowing a change in membership and, after that, the changes themselves. Some states also require you to inform them before adding or removing members.

Financial Prowess: Navigating LLC Finances

LLC finances are the resources you use to start, grow, and expand your business. These resources include assets, liabilities, income, expenses, and equity. Gaining financial prowess will help your business thrive from the onset. We discuss the most important aspects below.

Banking Brilliance: Your Guide to Business Accounts

An LLC business bank account helps to set up your company's financial presence in the market. The best account for an LLC goes a mile further in providing other services. For example, offering tools to simplify taxes and bookkeeping matters, refund or eliminate common fees, and offer you opportunities to receive money back on some business purchases.

Determine the accounts you need, such as savings, checking, or investment accounts. Remember to ask if they offer free employee debit cards, ATM rebates, or free wire transfers. The number of accounts you open depends on the size of your business and if you want to separate financial operations for easy accountability.

Cash Flow Mastery: Budgeting for Success

Budgeting for success requires you to keep comparing your company's revenue with the expenses incurred in a given period. Budgeting also helps you gauge your company's performance and know which areas need adjusting to maximize revenue. The following table outlines a variety of budgets you should consider having as you start your business.

Type of Budget	Use
Master budget	Financial projection for the entire company
Static budget	Contains planned financial outputs and inputs for various departments
Operating budget	Contains expenses and revenue from day-to-day operations
Cash-flow budget	Shows cash coming in and going out

Financial Tracking: Where Every Penny Goes

Most entrepreneurs struggle to track their expenses because it means taking intentional measures to trace where every penny goes. Technological advancement has simplified tracking your finances and everyday expenses. A business expense tracker helps to monitor your business's spending habits and simplifies record keeping and tax payments. Examples of expense trackers you can use are Expensify, Zoho Expense, Certify, MileIQ, and Concur Travel.

Tax Tactics: Planning and Payment Strategies

At the onset of your business, you may not feel the tax burden. But wait until your business grows. The various taxes, including federal and state income taxes and self-employment taxes, can increase to a frustrating level. Planning for taxes and adopting effective payment strategies can help you save money. **Some tax planning and payment strategies include:**

- Reduce your adjusted gross income by reducing your salary, signing up for a tax-deferred retirement plan or a health saving plan.

- Instead of increasing your employees' salary, offer fringe or tax-exempt benefits such as medical and dental insurance, child care assistance, transportation, and employee meals.

- Utilize carryover deductions such as capital losses, home office deductions, net operating losses, and charitable contributions.

- Postpone taxable income to future years. However, you may want to prepay important expenses before the year ends.

Staying ahead of your tax responsibilities also involves knowing the current small business tax laws and how they affect your business. Consulting a tax planner can also save you money and endless stress.

Documenting Your Journey: Records and Documentation

Every LLC must keep accurate records and documents from the onset. Documents such as the Articles of Organization and operating documents help the business have a reference point for its overall running needs. Other records and documents such as business licenses, meeting minutes, accounting books, tax registration, and membership certificates ensure you capture the finer details. Let's explore what you need to know about the paperwork.

The Gold Standard: Accurate Record-Keeping

Accurate record-keeping safeguards you against creditors and lawsuits that may try to exploit an area requiring record-keeping. Besides, an LLC's ability to offer limited liability also depends on keeping proper and factual records. You have no option but to find out your state's requirement for record-keeping and adhere to it. **Examples of records you need to keep accurately and track include:**

- Updated Articles of Organization

- All meeting minutes

- Amendments filed in your state

- Annual reports

- Names and addresses of managers and members

- Financial and accounting records

Consider using professionals from various fields to ensure you have accurate legal records that can stand in court or help you track your company's growth.

Organizing Chaos: Your Financial Records

Of all the records and documents you have to keep, financial records are the ones that change the most. So, it is not uncommon to find your financial records are disorganized. **Here are ways to ensure you organize the chaos you may find yourself in:**

1. Create a list of all the accounts you need to keep in a single folder

2. Create a system that tracks all income and expenses

3. Compare your office records to your bank statements

4. Have a plan on how you'll record depreciating assets

5. Hire someone to prepare and maintain all financial statements

The most efficient way to organize and keep accurate financial records is to use accounting software with provisions for most if not all, your financial needs. Examples are listed in this chapter under the "Financial Tracking: Where Every Penny Goes" section.

Ink It In: Documenting Agreements and Transactions

When starting and growing a business, you cannot afford to leave any interaction or communication to chance. From the beginning, have everything in writing and always have a section for signing.

Whether communicating with other members, lenders, managers, vendors, or co-owners, ensure all parties sign. Essential documents to have signatures on include articles of organization, the operating document, certificate of good standing, loan or credit approvals, business contacts, and deals.

Secure Vault: Digital Data and Record-Keeping

Technology has helped businesses save on office space needed to keep records and documents. Record keeping has been made easier and more efficient because you can keep all documents online. Be it contracts, meeting minutes, financial statements, or operating documents, you can access them within seconds and on a single screen.

The earlier concern for security has been addressed with advanced features such as user permission and encryption. We recommend embracing digital data storage to enhance your company's security for record-keeping, save time, and become more organized.

Compliance Chronicles: Regulations and Taxation

An LLC must remain compliant with the regulations specific to the business structure and the tax requirements expected at the state and federal levels. Failing to comply may lead to hefty fines, penalties, or loss of the LLC status. Let's look at what regulation and taxation entail in LLC compliance.

Taxes: Understanding Obligations

Understanding an LLC tax obligation depends on whether you registered it as a single-member or multiple-member LLC. Using income tax obligation as an illustration, a single-member LLC will prepare a Schedule C document (issued by the IRS) to report its net income. That figure will be forwarded to your personal tax return to be taxed as a sole proprietorship. Conversely, for multi-member income tax reporting, you will be taxed as a partnership. Each partner will fill out a Schedule K-1 and then transfer the information to a single Schedule E document. Finally, each partner transfers their net income to their personal income tax return.

Regulatory Compliance: The Key to LLC Health

Regulatory compliance determines your LLC's health because failure to remain compliant with federal, state, or local laws may cost you the business or the LLC brand. Compliance also helps to maintain accountability and transparency in the daily business operations. It ensures you are up-to-date with the shifting economy and market needs. Besides, if you are compliant, anyone seeking to sue you will have a harder time proving their case. Regularly conduct an LLC-compliant audit to maintain your LLC's health.

Reporting Reality: Annual Reports and Statements

Submitting an annual report for your LLC is a requirement in most states. This document should contain details of all your business activities in the previous year and your financial performance. The annual report must be submitted on the anniversary of your LLC formation or a specific date set by the state. Even though you have all the records for submission, you must visit your Secretary of State website and download an annual report form, fill it out, and submit it with the required attachments or send it via mail.

Sales Tax Simplified (if applicable)

Most states require you to collect sales taxes. However, some local authorities offer sales exemptions depending on the type of product and point of sale. As you start operations, you must know when and how to charge sales tax—following your state's requirements. After registration for sales tax collection, find an efficient method to document the sales tax collected daily, weekly, or monthly. As the filing date approaches, gather the entire sales tax record and file the returns according to your state's specifications.

Licenses and Permits Unleashed

Most businesses require more than one license to operate. The number you need depends on the type of business, state rules, and location. So, which ones do you need? We provide an answer below.

License Quest: Identifying Your Needs

Once you develop your vision, mission statement, and goals, you are probably sure of the business you want to conduct and the extent to which you will go. Using that information, you should identify your business needs and the licenses and permits you should acquire. **Examples that most businesses require include:**

- County permits for sensitive businesses

- State licenses for most occupations

- Federal licenses for businesses regulated by the federal government

- Specialty city permits if you use special materials that can be a risk to the public

Permit Power: Applying with Confidence

Acquiring a permit gives you the right to operate a business in a specific location [8]. It is a powerful document to have as it silences anyone who comes to dispute your right to operate in a particular locality or sell certain products or services. The power you'll receive from this document should encourage you to apply for it with confidence. As long as you've done your homework and followed our recommendation in this beginner guide, you should approach this task with assurance that you'll get the permit to operate your business.

Renewal Rhythms: Staying in Compliance

As you get your licenses and permits, confirm how often you need to renew. Some business permits and licenses do not need renewal once you get them; others have an expiration date and require you to apply for a new one, or you may have to close your business or pay fines. Every state and locality differs in how often you need to renew your licenses and permits. Some expire after one year, while others go for a longer period. Keep track of all the permits and licenses to stay compliant.

Local Legends: Industry-Specific Licensing

As the name implies, industry-specific licenses are those business licenses issued by industries specialized in an area of operation. These licenses ensure the person and the business meet particular criteria needed in that industry. For example, lawyers need certification from their state bar association. The federal, state, or private organizations (given a go-ahead by the state) issue the industry-specific licenses. Research carefully and ensure you meet all the requirements outlined.

Key Takeaways

- Members take full responsibility for the day-to-day running of the business in member-based LLCs, while managers perform the daily errands in manager-based LLCs.

- The best business bank account for an LLC offers tools to simplify tax and bookkeeping matters, refund or eliminate common fees, and provide opportunities to receive money back on some business purchases.

- Learning how to plan for taxes and adopting effective tax payment strategies will save you some money.

- Regulatory compliance determines your LLC's health because it helps to maintain accountability and transparency in daily business operations.

- Embrace digital data storage to enhance your company's security for record-keeping, save time, and become more organized.

- Some business permits and licenses do not need renewal once you get them, while others have an expiration date and require you to apply for a new one.

Chapter 5

Financing and Funding Your LLC

"Money is like gasoline during a road trip. You don't want to run out of gas on your trip, but you're not doing a tour of gas stations."
-Tim O'Reilly

Launching Your Business Finances

You entered into business to make money, but you must use what you already have well before you hit the target you had in mind. Having a business idea, identifying a target market, and noticing a need you can meet is not enough to realize your dream. You need money to put things in motion. Let's look at how to do it right.

Unmasking Startup Costs: Unveiling the Initial Expenses

Before choosing the method to finance your business, you must calculate how much money you will likely need for startup costs and unavoidable expenses. The initial step is to list all the expenses you will likely incur before and after you start operations. **The following table categorizes these expenses and gives you examples.**

Type of Expense	Examples
One time expenses	Equipment, machinery, or vehicles Incorporation fees Permits and licenses Computer or technology equipment Initial inventory and office supplies
Ongoing expenses	Utilities Marketing materials Office Supplies and operating expenses Website hosting and maintenance Business taxes
Fixed expenses	Lease or mortgage Insurance Utilities Administrative costs
Variable expenses	Inventory Payroll Shipping Packaging

Navigating Year One: Estimating Operational Costs

Once you've created a list of all the expenses you will incur, it's time to research and get the average cost of each item. For example, consult the registration agency to determine how much you need to register an LLC and get the necessary licenses. Shop around for the office equipment, furniture, and supplies you need, and take the most affordable ones. Further, set a certain percentage aside for other expenses like business taxes and utility charges that you may not know exactly how much you'll spend until the end of the month or quarter.

Safety Net Essentials: Contingency Planning for Unexpected Expenses

Regardless of how well you research and get your estimates, always expect to experience some setbacks or delays that may require you to use more cash. Factor in these unforeseeable expenses by adding cushion money. Some ongoing expenses may also increase as the months progress, so have some amount in the budget for these additional expenses.

Besides, it is important to ensure you have enough money to sustain the business for 6 to 12 months without expecting the business to fund itself. This is not to say that your business will not make money, but at this point, you cannot predict your sales until you start operating for a few months.

Funding Expedition: Your Path to Capital

Your financial strategy is in place, and you know where the money will go as you open your doors for business. Now, you need to have the money in your pocket to get started. Funding your LLC requires you to pull money from various avenues [9]. The following sections explore four sources.

Self-Funding and Bootstrapping: Starting Lean and Strong

The first place to look into to fund your business should be your own finances. New entrepreneurs often get money to start by liquidating their assets or using their possessions as collateral for loans. You may also go to the extent of using your personal savings or selling your property.

However, you must be careful when you dive deep into your personal assets. You risk losing your possessions if your business fails and you have taken a loan with your home, car, or land. To reduce the risk of losing your personal belongings if things go south, plan to make regular payments back to yourself. The main advantage of self-funding is that you have complete control of the business and do not have to answer to investors.

The Borrower's Route: Unraveling Debt Financing (Loans & Credit)

The traditional route of applying for loans from credit unions and banks is also an alternative to funding your LLC. Unfortunately, most lenders are reluctant to give their money to new businesses. So, be prepared to be rejected on multiple occasions. However, you can improve your chances of getting the loan by including your assets as collateral. LLC's safety net of having limited personal liability protects you from creditors accessing your assets if you fail to make the loan payments.

Another relatively similar way of getting a loan is through peer-to-peer lending websites. These online platforms allow you to apply for a loan.

Afterward, interested institutions or individuals decide whether to lend you the money and pay it back at an agreed interest rate. Examples of these sites are Prosper, Funding Circle, and Upstart.

The Investor's Pitch: Equity Financing (Angel Investors & VC)

Looking for individuals or entities to invest in your company and relinquish a percentage of your ownership is a route many entrepreneurs use to kick-start their business or grow it to new heights. Two main options for equity financing are looking for angel investors or venture capitalists.

Angel investors usually give a lower amount for a smaller percentage of the company, while venture capitalists offer more money, and you must give a higher percentage of your business. In addition, angel investors come in to help in the early days of your business, while venture capitalists come in later when they see your company has undeniable potential for growth.

A Crowd-Pleasing Alternative: Crowdfunding and More

Crowdfunding as a funding option entails asking people to donate to your LLC either online (Kickstarter or Indiegogo) or in person. Online tends to work better because you have a wider reach of people who may be willing to support you. You not only ask for money but also promise a reward for some, if not most, of your fund supporters.

To succeed with this approach, you must have a captivating marketing approach. You must also keep in mind that you may not get all the money you need for the startup. In most sites, you must wait until the crowdfunding campaign is over to access the funds. Use this approach if all other fundraising options are not available to you.

The Art of Bootstrapping

Can you start a successful business without relying on outside investments other than your personal finances? As business owners who have actually done it, we believe you can. Bootstrapping requires you to maximize the finances you already have to start and run your business. Here are the ways you can do it right.

Thrifty Tactics: Strategies for a Frugal Beginning

As you think of bootstrapping, consider carefully how your business will run with limited funds for the first few months of operations. Do not overcommit the little funds you have or overpromise your potential customers. **The following are strategies to implement:**

- Create a business plan with a very specific financial budget

- Determine how your revenue will cycle back to the business before paying yourself back

- Establish where additional resources will come from. For example, your own cash, borrow from your personal line of credit or use your time instead of employing someone.

- Plan to limit business operations. For example, only produce products upon order.

Penny-Wise Promotion: Cost-Effective Marketing

Working with a tight budget requires you to refine your marketing strategies. You want to get your business out there and become well-known, but do so in a way that'll have a high ROI for your business. To save on marketing, you need to consider the four main areas that can be affected by marketing and how to approach them. Let's illustrate with a table.

Marketing Aspect	What to Consider	Result
Product	Producing a good quality product or service with features that meet the customers' needs	The product or service will sell itself without over-advertising
Price	Choose a price that is not too high but also not too low to prevent you from making a profit	The product or service will sell itself without over-advertising
Place	Find out where your potential customers are and advertise on those platforms	Reach more people with less expenses compared to non-specific advertising
Promotion	Know what will captivate your potential customer and do exactly that.	More effective marketing with a targeted approach

Dollars and Sense: Efficient Resource Management

Efficient resource management ensures all the resources are used correctly and for the right projects or needs. Scrutinizing how the financial resources are used ensures you achieve your objectives even with limited funding available. **You accomplish this by:**

- Having all the information on a centralized platform to get a holistic approach and notice gaps.

- Assigning available resources to areas that need immediate attention.

- Distributing your resources across all areas instead of focusing on one area.

- Checking if there are new and more affordable resources to meet the same business need at a lower cost.

Tightening the Purse Strings: Mastering Cash Flow

To master cash flow, you need to know what happened to your LLC's money last month and what will happen to your cash in the coming days. This ensures you notice when you start bleeding cash and what you can do to recover. For instance, you'll know when to negotiate with your customers to make payments earlier than they want to commit. Or ask lenders to allow you to delay payments until a certain future date.

Attracting Angels and VC Wizards

As you seek to bring in investors, remember that not everyone who shows you the money is a great fit for your business. You first need to understand your business and the target market to know the kind of investor who will add value to it. Let's discuss how to win over the right investors.

Crafting a Captivating Pitch Deck

A pitch that captivates the investors highlights what you do, why you differ from similar businesses, and the problem you'll solve. You can also factor in brief financial figures and what customers or potential customers have said about your business. You may need to craft several pitch versions specific to various audiences, and always have a short 60-second point at your fingertips in case of an impromptu presentation.

Hunting for Investment Gold: Prospective Investors

As you try to find investors, you might realize that many focus on specific needs such as a business structure, industry, or under-represented founders. Regardless of the business they pick, they want to make revenue. They may not write big checks as from the start, but if you choose carefully, you can get investors to mentor you in running a successful business. However, they will not be involved in the daily LLC operations. **You can find these investors through:**

- Referrals and introductions

- Strategic networking

- Industry conferences and seminars

- Online investment platforms

- Cold outreach

The Art of Negotiation: Terms and Agreements

Investors seek to partner with someone who is not only after their money but is passionate about the business they are venturing into.

If possible, learn about the investor you are about to negotiate with and brainstorm some questions they might ask. When you enter the negotiating room [10], **do not:**

- Be quick to speak and preempt your terms.

- Assume you know what they mean; instead, ask questions to clarify.

- Overlook using your strengths as leverage.

- Use tricks or lies to win them over.

- Settle for less than you think your business is worth.

Sealing the Deal: Due Diligence and Closure

As with any important document, you must ensure that what you have in writing is what you agreed to in the meeting. Request more time to review the agreement you crafted with the investor during negotiations. Seek a lawyer's opinion to review the document or assist with amending the new agreement. You can also ask the investor for another meeting to discuss and clarify any ambiguous clauses. After that, confirm everything and sign the contract.

Leveraging Loans and Grants

Exploring loans or grants when starting your company or surviving a turbulent season is a viable option. The only difference between the two is that loans require repayments, whereas grants are one-time funding that you obtain from the government and non-profit organizations. Let's explore the vital aspects to know about loans and grants.

The Quest for Financing: Researching Options

Once you decide to either apply for a loan or a grant or use both methods, it is necessary to conduct relevant research on which lenders or grantors would be ready to give you the money. Look for unique grant opportunities targeted at your industry or those that your business will successfully address a need the government or NGO desires to meet. To get started, search online and in your locality for available grants in relation to your sector, tell your contacts about your plan to apply, and learn more from former grant recipients.

Paperwork Precision: Crafting Loan Applications and Proposals

Putting your thoughts, desires, and needs on paper can be more challenging than you think. You can put so much in the application proposal that you may be confused about what to add or leave. Don't worry, we got you covered. **Here are the five elements you need to add to your loan application or proposal:**

- Begin by giving an exhaustive description of your business and current financial situation.

- Explain why you need the loan and how it will assist you in meeting your goals.

- List assets you will include as collateral or security against the loan.

- Explain in detail how you plan to pay them back.

- Attach all supporting documents about your LLC, taxes, asset vs liability net ratio, balanced sheets, and bank statements.

Most grants do not require you to pay back the money, so you don't need to add a section on collateral assets or repayment plans, but you must include an exhaustive needs assessment, project description, and detailed budget.

Meeting the Requirements: Navigating Loan and Grant Expectations

Since loans are easier to get than grants, you are likely to get the loan approved if you add a collateral asset compared to not including any. Grants, on the other hand, are harder to get, so you must have an open mind. If you receive approval, the grant-giving agency will give you guidelines on how to use the funds and report its use. Loan lenders do not follow up on how you use the money as long as you repay them.

Financial Responsibility: Managing Repayments and Reporting

Loan repayments are usually straightforward because it entails keeping to what you agreed to in the contract and making timely payments. Ensure you do not miss payments or default because it will ruin your LLC's reputation with other lenders. In grant reporting, you are required to give a summarized narrative of the specific business project and a detailed financial report.

Ensure you provide the information you agreed to submit in the grant agreement you signed. Any changes from the original agreement should be reflected within the narrative section. Additionally, the narrative and the financial report should agree. For example, you cannot report you sold to 800 customers, and your sales report shows 920.

Key Takeaways

- Regardless of how well you research and get your budget estimates, always expect to experience some setbacks or delays that may require you to use more money.

- Most lenders are reluctant to give their money to new businesses. However, you can improve your chances of getting the loan by including your assets as collateral.

- Scrutinizing how the financial resources are used ensures you achieve your objectives even with limited funding.

- A pitch that captivates the investors highlights what you do, why you differ from similar businesses, and the problem you'll solve.

- Search for grants online or in your community, contact your networks to inform them of your plan, and talk to previous grant recipients about available opportunities.

Chapter 6

Nurturing Your LLC for Growth

"Test, measure, learn. It is the best way to understand what works best for your company and invest in the right area to become more efficient and achieve business growth."

-Irina Georgieva

Scaling Your LLC

After your business becomes a success and you are hitting your targets and meeting your goals, it is time to consider expanding. To succeed at scaling your business, you must ask yourself if you have the capacity to grow and to accommodate the growth. We will help you assess yourself and the business in this section.

Crafting Your Path to Sustainable Growth

Nurturing sustainable growth means that your business can support itself. It should give you reasonable profits, meet your customers' needs, and provide the employees with the support they need. **The following are steps you can apply at an early stage to avoid serious scaling mistakes:**

- Understand the changing customer needs and innovate to meet them.

- Implement well-defined processes addressing the rising needs.

- Monitor the changing industry dynamics and adopt or adjust as needed.

- Improve customer experience as the numbers increase.

- Ruthlessly monitor operations as targets and goals shift.

- Provide a healthy company culture with strong communication channels.

- Model integrity, honesty, and flexibility as the founder and business owner.

As you focus on these elements, remember to create brand loyalty so that your customers can stick by you even during challenging economic times.

Expanding Your Footprint: Products, Services, and Markets

Expanding your footprint involves creating a plan of action that will enable your business to grow its operations, add to its market share, and achieve the new scaling goals. Business expansion covers selling more of your products or services and entering new markets.

Expanding to new markets entails going into different geographical areas and opening new stores or establishing an online presence. Expansion in terms of products and services can involve creating a new product or service, licensing your product to other businesses, partnering with other companies, or repackaging your product or service to widen the reach.

Power Moves: Building Strategic Alliances and Partnerships

Strategic alliances and partnerships occur when two or more companies agree to work on a project together that will be of benefit to both parties. You may choose to enter such an arrangement to enable you to improve or sell more products or services, expand into a new market, or place yourself in a better position than your competitors [11].

Steps to form an alliance or partnership include brainstorming the kind of partners you'd like, how you'll approach the conversation, and drafting an alliance proposal that clearly shows how both parties will benefit. Once you get a company that agrees to the proposal, determine the goals together and devise a fair, profitable, and sustainable plan.

Crafting a Blueprint for Growth

When you launched your business, you created a blueprint for your startup. You ensured it captured your business needs and goals and had a strategic growth plan. Now, your business is growing, and you need to go back to the drawing board and create a new one or adjust the existing one to have a better business framework that will accommodate your growing business. We captured what you need to work on below.

Navigating Growth: SWOT Analysis and Strategy

In chapter two, we explained the meaning of SWOT analysis and outlined its parts in a table showing what each letter stands for and how it affects your business. You should also perform the same process with your growing business. Look at the strengths you've acquired over time. What are the weaknesses that are now preventing you from expanding more, which new and different opportunities are coming up as you grow, and what threats are you experiencing that will hinder you from further growth? Brainstorm and analyze these factors, then come up with a strategy to address each part.

Setting Sights on Success: Growth Goals and Milestones

It is often said that goals without milestones lack direction. Indeed, if you do not set clear milestones after you come up with your goals for the growing business, you will likely underachieve. Milestones are indicators that give you a picture of the growth process and help simplify your goals and objectives into manageable and easily identified day-to-day activities. After developing your goals, the milestones for each should contain four elements: description, date, budget, and delegation. These four elements will help you create clear and accurate direction for your team.

Turning Strategy into Action: Implementing and Monitoring Growth

Implementing and monitoring your growing business is the next step after developing a new business plan with specific goals and milestones. Implementation involves doing the work, while monitoring refers to measuring or tracking the numbers behind the implemented strategy. Below is a table that provides five ways of monitoring your business.

Monitoring Method	How it's Done
Live monitoring and testing	Looking at the live performance and the numbers as it happens
Reviews	Asking the customers about their experience with your business

Analytics Tools	Asking the customers about their experience with your business
Meetings and Appraisals	Asking the team directly about their views or analyzing individual performance
Market research	Comparing your current sales with the previous ones or with competitors

Adapt and Thrive: Fine-Tuning Strategies for Optimal Results

The first step in fine-tuning your business strategies is making sure you know everything about your new growth plan and how you wish to implement it. **The following are examples of fine-tuning strategies you can use to ensure optimal results in your business:**

- Refine your business goals and value proposition

- Enhance financial management

- Streamline operations and processes

- Evaluate competition and market trends

- Strengthen your sales and marketing approach

Getting optimal results for your business is not a one-time task. You have to keep monitoring, evaluating, and adjusting until you meet your target.

Beyond Borders and Boundaries

Doing business across states and internationally has been simplified by technology and efficient modern-day travel options. Even though logistically, things look manageable to expand beyond borders and boundaries. You must consider some key factors to succeed in it. Let's discuss more about it.

Franchise Fever: Taking Your Brand Nationwide

Taking your brand nationwide is a big step in your business journey that is worth celebrating. However, you must think through it carefully to ensure the timing is right and the approach will favor your success. **Here are some steps to consider as you think about franchising:**

- Find out what drove you to consider expanding.

- Generate a tailored strategy that would work in a new location

- Create a schedule of activities and add timelines

- Create an appealing portfolio of your products or services

- Open accounts at the new location

Locations, Locations, Locations: The Art of Expansion

The location where you intend to operate plays an essential role in determining whether the business will grow immediately after opening. The site you pick should be dictated by the kind of business you are engaged in and your own needs. **The following are tips to help you choose the right location:**

- Choose a location that fits your budget

- Factor in the location of the potential suppliers and vendors Establish your store where your products and services are in demand

- Consider transportation and accessibility for your employees

- Choose a safe location with ample spaces to park

Branching Out: Diversifying Your Offerings

Diversification is about making your presence felt in a new place after offering your products or services and increasing your profits in the process. Diversification can take several forms. For instance, you can diversify horizontally by introducing a new product or service to the market. The product can be in line with what you already offer or a totally different product with no relation to what you have. Vertical diversification entails adding a product that relates to what you already offer. For example, a salon offering hair services can decide to add a section for selling hair products.

Worldwide Ambitions: Considerations for Global Expansion

Expanding worldwide is a whole different ball game that requires you to take all precautionary measures before embarking on that journey. The following table presents the factors to consider before expanding globally.

Global Expansion Factor to Consider	What it Entails
Affordability	Include additional expenses such as international travel and customs

Employment and tax requirements	Different countries have their own requirements for employment and taxation regulations
Currency	Trade rate may fluctuate, making it hard to fix your costs to the international conversion scale
Financial and political unpredictability	Can make or break your new business when a serious crisis occurs in another country

Your marketing strategies will also change to align with the culture and preferences of the new region. You may need to form local partnerships from the onset to get it right.

Building a Winning Team

Building a winning team is a challenging process that requires commitment and a desire to invest in people. Merely having a group of talented employees does not automatically make them a winning team. You must put additional effort into the entire recruiting and retention process. We will discuss how you can build a winning team below.

Scouting Talent: Recruiting and Hiring the Right Way

Recruiting and hiring the right people is a critical task for ensuring adequate business growth. The right team ensures the company reaches its targets in terms of growth, maximizes productivity, provides better customer services, and enhances creative ideas. **Follow these steps to increase your chances of getting the right team:**

1. Outline your hiring requirements and create a precise job description.

2. Advertise on the most appropriate job posting site or work with a recruiting company.

3. Go through resumes and focus on who stands out.

4. Create a unique interview plan and ask the questions that matter to you.

5. Contact the references and perform background checks.

6. Choose the most appealing candidate and make an offer.

7. Onboard the new team member after negotiating the salary.

Onboarding Excellence: Setting Employees Up for Success

When you onboard new employees well, you set them up for success when they connect with coworkers, have a better grasp of the workplace culture, and get a deeper understanding of their new responsibilities. **To ensure you get these three variables right, here are factors to have in place:**

- Connecting them with relevant and friendly mentors during onboarding

- Ensuring the manager or supervisor is present and helpful

- Introducing them to employees on their department or floor

- Assigning someone to show them how things work

- Asking for feedback to know when they feel isolated or confused

Keeping Stars in Your Constellation: Employee Retention

Employee retention occurs when your hired team chooses not only to stay in your company but is also not actively looking for another job. When you keep talents for longer, you are able to maintain uninterrupted business flow, enhance productivity, and reduce the costs of hiring. To retain your employees, you must give them challenging work, train them in other disciplinary skills as they hone their core skills, and develop a succession plan with them. You can encourage poor performers to step up by identifying why they are performing poorly and addressing the skills gap immediately.

Playing by the Rules: Legal Compliance and HR Mastery

Ensuring your company remains legally compliant in terms of human affairs requires you to have HR mastery. This means working with an HR manager who pays close attention to matters like recruitment, productivity, and retention [12]. They also monitor the employment laws to ensure your company adheres to all guidelines, including payroll, benefits, risk and safety, hiring, employee relations, and termination.

However, early on as your business grows, you may need to handle the HR duties yourself.

Adapting and Thriving

As seasoned business owners, we can confirm that your business will face a few shake-ups, be it from new regulations, the competitive landscape, or a national crisis. You need to learn from an early stage how to adapt to changes. We will explain more in the following paragraphs.

Market Watch: Staying Ahead of Trends and Shifts

A key area you must monitor to stay ahead is your market. The changes in the market include changing customer habits, the evolving business environment, and innovations that may threaten or improve your business. For example, artificial intelligence is here to stay, and you must keep innovating and finding creative ideas that you can work along with it or rise above it with the human qualities it lacks. Anticipating shifts and noticing new trends will help you make strategic decisions, such as training employees to acquire the skills to adapt to the change, improving the product or service, and looking for partnerships for reinforcement.

Flexible Foundations: Pivoting Your Business Model

Pivoting your business models involves changing an aspect of your company after realizing your product or services fail to meet the current or emerging needs of the market. Pivoting can help your company survive in the market and improve your revenue. Selcuk Atli, Co-founder of Bunch, came up with five pivoting areas that follow a standard order.

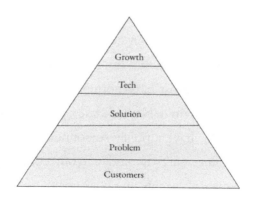

Selcuk asserts that pivoting requires you to understand if the customers are the issue (targeting the wrong group), you misinterpreted the problem you are trying to solve with your product or services, you are offering the wrong solution to the right or wrong problem, and your technology choice is working against your business. Once you address the factor causing a challenge, you'll experience growth.

Crisis Control: Navigating Stormy Waters with Grace

Whether you plan for it or not, a crisis is likely to occur at some point in your LLC. It may be internal (among members or employees) or external (with vendors, customers, or state regulators). To navigate the stormy waters with grace, you must put in place a crisis management plan that outlines who will take action when a specific crisis occurs and what their role entails. The goal of dealing with any crisis is to limit the harm done and restore normal business operations. Once you realize there is a crisis, pick a team to assess the crisis and determine the impact. Afterward, devise a plan for response, implement it, review it, and adjust until the crisis is over.

Lessons from the School of Hard Knocks: Gaining Wisdom from Failures

Failing in business is often inevitable. You will try some things and realize they don't work, or you may even make a loss from it. But failing provides a learning experience that can help you succeed. Keep in mind that when you fail, you must have gotten something wrong. Find out what it was, and research on it. Next, devise a plan to recover and ensure you train your team or have a policy surrounding it to avoid the same mistake. Indeed, failure isn't the end of your company. It is a slight setback on your journey to achieving your goals.

Key Takeaways

- Nurturing sustainable growth means that your business can support itself by making reasonable profits and meeting customers' needs.

- Milestones are indicators that give you a picture of the growth process and help simplify your goals and objectives into manageable and easily identified day-to-day activities.

- Diversification can be done horizontally by introducing a new product or service to the market or vertically by adding a product that relates to what you already offer.

- To retain your employees, you must give them challenging work, train them in other disciplinary skills, and develop a succession plan with them.

- To navigate a crisis, you must have a crisis management plan that outlines who will take action when a specific crisis occurs and what their role entails.

Chapter 7

Navigating LLC Taxes

"The legal right of a taxpayer to decrease the amount of what otherwise would be his taxes, or altogether to avoid them, by means which the law permits, cannot be doubted."
-George Sutherland

Deciphering Tax Complexity: LLCs Unveiled

A primary reason business prefer starting as an LLC is the tax benefit that comes with it. Unlike corporations, LLC permits business owners to pay taxes once. This section explains this advantage and discusses other critical tax information.

Unraveling Pass-Through Taxation

Pass-through taxation occurs when an entrepreneur pays taxes on LLC income after it is distributed to the owners as wages or an investment return. This means that each LLC member must report the company's income and losses on their personal income tax return. In the IRS records, an LLC is treated as a disregarded entity for tax purposes, meaning the LLC has no obligation to pay taxes and does not exist outside the owners.

Slight variation occurs in the method of taxation depending on whether the LLC is a single-member or a multi-member. An LLC owned by one person pays taxes as a sole proprietorship and reports income and losses on personal tax returns. While an LLC with multiple owners can be taxed as a partnership, corporation, or S-corporation. The default method is a partnership.

Unveiling the Self-Employment Tax Quandary

Apart from your regular income tax, you are required to pay self-employment tax. For instance, as an employee, you would pay half of the Social Security and Medicare taxes and your employer the other half. But as a self-employed person, you must pay the entire amount.

Fortunately, there's a way to reduce the tax burden. Once you set up an LLC, you can choose to exist as a disregarded LLC and pay the self-employment taxes in full or elect to be taxed as an S-Corporation, which reduces the burden of paying self-employment tax. As an S-Corp, you pay yourself a salary, and the self-employment taxes will be deducted from there. Afterward, pay yourself other amounts as distributions from the S-Corp. This approach prevents you from paying self-employment taxes on that amount.

Tax Credits and Deductions Demystified

Interestingly, the IRS does not typically tax an LLC directly. Instead, profits are paid to members, who then file them on their personal tax returns. This is called pass-through taxation. Members then file personal income taxes, including the profits from the LLC. However, LLCs offer an advantage in flexible tax classification.

An LLC is not limited to pass-through taxation but can elect to file as an S corporation. If the LLC is classified as an S corporation, the LLC files a tax return as a separate entity. IRS Form 8832 Entity Class Election allows you to change the tax classification of the LLC. The benefits of an S corp classification include savings on Medicare and Social Security taxes since members gain employee status. This also allows members to avoid self-employment taxes. However, it may pose a double taxation issue as the LLC pays a corporate tax rate, and members pay personal income taxes on the income from the LLC. An experienced tax advisor can help you decide which tax status is best for your individual situation.

Mastery of Business Taxes: A Strategic Approach

Once you know how to lower the tax burden, the next step is mastering the taxation process, even if that means outsourcing to a tax professional. You can opt to take care of the tax requirements and obligations on your own or employ a tax professional to do it. Either way, the following section addresses what you need to know.

Tax Time Tactics: Filing for Your LLC

Filing taxes for your LLC depends on whether you are a single or multi-member LLC. **The main difference is the IRS forms used. Let's look at the steps:**

1. Prepare all the documents and have them ready.

2. Choose the right tax form. For a single-member LLC, you will use Schedule C. Add the income and expenses from the business in the form, then transfer the income or loss on your personal tax return Form 1040.

3. For multi-member LLCs, you must complete Form 1065 for partnerships and Form 1120-S for an S-Corp. Afterward, you must

provide a Schedule K-1 to each member. They should calculate their percentage income and transfer it to their personal tax return forms.

4. Next, fill out Schedule SE, which covers your self-employment taxes.

5. Calculate state and federal employment taxes if you have employees.

6. Consider any other state-applicable taxes.

The Art of Anticipating Quarterly Tax Payments

As a member of a business that operates as an LLC, you will likely owe quarterly taxes. Small businesses pay this type of tax in advance of their annual tax return. It operates on a pay-as-you-go basis where you pay throughout the year as estimations. **Two main guidelines used to confirm whether you qualify to make quarterly tax payments are:**

-   You will owe more than $1,000 (after tax credit) when filing your return at the end of the year.

-   Your withholding and tax credits will likely be less than 90% of your tax liability for the year.

Depending on what type of LLC you have - if you're a single member LLC, 1120S, or a Form 1065, you'll take that income and use it to calculate your quarterly income taxes on a Form 1040-ES. You're expected to file four times a year.

Deadlines and Extensions: Staying One Step Ahead

The deadline for paying your personal taxes from your LLC's income is April 15. However, if you elect to be taxed as a C-Corp or S-Corp, you must file your annual returns by March 15. Since you may also have quarterly payments, the deadline is as follows: April 15, June 15, September 15, and lastly, January 15.

The IRS penalizes you for filing late and failing to pay on time, even after filing before the deadline. Fortunately, the IRS allows you to file for an extension using Form 4868, but you must make the request before the tax return due date. If approved, you will receive an extension of six months. The IRS also allows you to get an extension by paying part or all of your income tax due and informing them that it's for an extension.

Tax Pro vs. DIY: Making the Right Choice

After interacting with the above information, you may feel overwhelmed by the requirements and forms needed to manage your taxes. You should consider hiring a professional to ease the burden if you have several sources of income and sizable assets. But if you have one stream of income and little to no deduction, then DIY is possible once you understand the requirements. Assess your situation and determine if DIY or hiring a tax professional will save you money in the long run.

Balancing the Books: The Accounting Odyssey

Balancing the books is the ultimate determinant of whether your business is worth remaining open. You can tell the general financial health of your company by looking at the financial records and transactions. So, what is involved in bookkeeping? We answer this question below.

Precise Financial Records: A Keystone for Success

Keeping precise financial records helps you assess your business profitability. It enables you to identify where your financial weaknesses and strengths lie. This action helps you to make informed decisions on investments, budgeting, and future growth strategies. **The following are other ways accurate financial records set you up for success:**

- Assist you in remaining tax compliant.

- Establish organizational trust and transparency.

- Ensure you detect fraud and errors.

- Keep you organized and efficient.

Cash vs. Accrual: The Accounting Dilemma

As a small business owner, you have the option of using cash or an accrual accounting system. The main difference is that accrual accounting registers expenses and revenue when a transaction occurs and without payment, while cash accounting registers the expenses and revenue when cash exchanges hands. The table below summarizes the key differences.

Cash Accounting	Accrual accounting
Records after receiving money	Records after a transaction
Less accurate for not recognizing unpaid items	More accurate as it gives an overall picture of business transactions

Ease to use	Complex because of multiple records for tracking payments
Preferred by small businesses	Serves larger companies better because of inventory

The Ledger Landscape: DIY or Pro?

Without a doubt, a general ledger can be a complex book to keep. It contains all your company's classified financial data and is recorded as debits and credits. It has various financial accounts such as owner's equity, assets, liabilities, revenues, and expenses. Do you think you can manage to keep up with all this information? It is possible for a small business, but if your business has undergone significant growth, hiring a professional accountant can save you time and energy and eventually save you some money when they streamline your accounts.

Tools of the Trade: Accounting Software Insights

Manual methods of tracking finances are no longer ideal in today's world. Lots of accounting software has been developed for small and large businesses. Using this software helps reduce human errors in record keeping, inventory, budgeting, and when handling account payables and receivables. These tools include Wave, Zoho, QuickBooks, FreshBooks, Xero, and Sage.

Dollars and Deductions: A Tax Odyssey

The IRS legally allows businesses to take advantage of available provisions that can save companies thousands of dollars through tax deductions. Make it part of your goal to learn about tax deductions and use them every time you file your taxes.

Tax Benefits Unveiled: Common LLC Deductions

As mentioned earlier, you can take advantage of tax deductions using various provisions that the IRS approves. These deductions are used to encourage businesses to grow and enable them to add benefits specific to employees without incurring additional costs in taxes. **The following are examples of LLC deductions you can explore:**

- Starting a business expenses

- Home office expenses

- Travel and vehicle expenses

- Business meals

- Education and medical expenses

- Business interest, bank fees, and insurance

- Rent expenses

- Professional Expenses

- Certain office supplies and utilities

Exploring the Frontier: R&D Tax Credits

The Research and Development (R&D) tax credit can be claimed by companies dedicated to coming up with new and improved business elements such as computer software, products, techniques, formulas, or inventions [15]. As a start-up, you can apply for the R&D tax credit against your payroll for up to five years. **Your business could be eligible if you:**

- Improve on existing products.

- Use your time and resources to produce new and innovative products.

- Come up with patents, prototypes, processes, or software.

- Hire scientists, designers, and engineers.

Opportunities Unlocked: The Work Opportunity Tax Credit (WOTC)

The Federal government offers the Work Opportunity Tax Credit (WOTC) to employers who hire people from a particular targeted group undergoing significant employment barriers. You can qualify to claim the **WOTC for a person who falls under the following category of people:**

- Formerly incarcerated or convicted of felony.

- Veterans.

- Resident of empowerment zones or rural renewal counties.

- A rehabilitated person.

- A person whose family is under state assistance or supplemental security income.

The Home Office Advantage: Deduction Details

As the name implies, home office deduction permits entrepreneurs doing business at their residential premises to deduct certain home expenses on their tax returns. **These expenses include:**

- Mortgage interest

- Utilities

- Repairs

- Maintenance

- Depreciation

- Rent

To qualify, you must be exclusively using a part of your home for operating your business regularly. Secondly, the home must be your principal place of running your business. However, if you have another location but conduct your administrative and management activities at home, you may still benefit from a home office deduction.

Expertise Beyond DIY: Tapping into Financial Professionals

Reaching this far into the guide, you may have noticed that you have significant work to do to get your LLC up and running. Not forgetting the changes you must implement as your company grows. The question on your mind could be, will you single-handedly manage all these tasks, or do you need to look for professionals? As you think about it, we will outline what you need to know about working with professionals.

Partnering with the Pros: Accountants and CPAs

At some point in your business, you will need to hire an accountant or a CPA to manage your financial records. They can also assist you in planning your LLC business structure from the beginning. Having an accountant coming on board will help to keep complex tax information in check. The following table shows other duties a CPA or accountant can perform.

Accountant/CPA's Function	Benefit
Tax advice and planning	Save money on taxes and keep track of new legislation impacting taxation for your business
Management and consulting	Budgeting, preparing statements, and risk management
Audit and assurance	Addresses tax problems
Payroll administration	Ensures everyone is paid on time
Bookkeeping	Handles account receivables and invoices
Forensic accounting	Prevent or discover embezzlement or fraud

Financial Advisors: Your Trusted Navigator

The descriptor of "financial advisor" encompasses various financial professionals who can help your business succeed. A financial advisor can be an investment manager, stockbroker, financial planner, tax preparer, estate planner, and banker [16]. Generally, the financial advisor you work with should provide advice and guidance on a specific financial matter. They should be well-educated, experienced, and have the proper credentials. The person you choose should work on your behalf to ensure your business achieves its goals while maximizing its revenue.

Legal and Tax Gurus: Consultants for Clarity

A business that desires to stay compliant and take advantage of available legal and tax benefits must consult with an attorney or tax professional at some point. **An experienced business attorney can assist you in:**

- Creating and enforcing contracts.

- Ensuring asset, property, and cash protection.

- Preparing employment agreements.

- Enlightening you on tax laws.

- Guiding you on the closure of LLC or bankruptcy application.

A tax consultant comes in to guide you through tax return preparation and filing. They will also assist you to claim the deductions mentioned earlier. A tax guru will help you discover all the secrets the IRS makes it difficult for most businesses to know. The IRS has targets to meet, and they count on a complex tax code "hiding" some tax advantages and loopholes.

Empowering DIY: Resources for Financial Mastery

The DIY approach to operating and managing your business will be effective if you remain focused and organized. Financial stability and a positive cash flow are signs that you are going in the right direction. **Tasks you need to add to your to-do list include:**

- Budgeting

- Tax planning

- Forecasting

- Accounting

- Risk management

Don't let this list intimidate you. Diverse resources are available to simplify your work. They include accounting software like Quickbooks and Square, payroll software like Square Automatic Payroll, income tax software like TaxCloud and EasyOffice, and management tools like Monday.com and Wrike.

Key Takeaways

- The state or federal government does not require the LLC to pay taxes, but it passes through to the members' individual tax returns. However, some states, like Rhode Island, have an annual tax that must be paid.

- The members of an LLC are likely to owe quarterly taxes, depending upon the income received from the LLC.

- Keeping precise financial records helps you assess your business profitability and identify where your financial weaknesses and strengths lie.

- R&D (research and development) tax credit can be claimed by companies dedicated to coming up with new and improved business elements such as computer software, products, techniques, formulas, or inventions.

- A financial advisor can be an investment manager, stockbroker, financial planner, tax preparer, estate planner, banker, and accountant. They should provide advice and guidance on a specific financial matter.

Chapter 8

Navigating Transitions and Beyond

> "In business, you don't get what you deserve; you get what you negotiate."
> -Dr. Chester L. Karass

Selling Your LLC: The Art of Transition

What happens when you reach a point in your LLC where you feel it's time to sell? You can get to this point when you are approached with a good deal, you want to pursue a new venture, or you just want to retire. Selling your LLC needs careful planning and creating a business blueprint for a seamless transition. We look at how to go about it in this section.

Preparing Your LLC for Sale: Getting It Market-Ready

Ensuring your LLC is ready for sale involves studying your business and getting it market-ready. That means you must evaluate where buyers are at regarding service features and then add any missing elements to enhance the value of your company. **The following are essential elements to work on to make your LLC market-ready:**

- Evaluate your LLC's position by examining the financial statements.

- Evaluate the current market condition and improve your financial performance.
- Look into your existing working relationships and strengthen the bond.
- Analyze your competitors and how you can stay ahead.

Valuing Your Business: What's It Really Worth?

You define what you consider to be the worth of your business by assessing all areas of the company: capital structure, management, net book value (market value of assets), and net profit or loss. These factors estimate your company's value and assist you at the negotiation table. The three methods available for valuing your business are summarized in the table below.

Valuation Approach	How its Done
Asset-based approach	Gives a total of all your investments, determining your business' value. It's done by adding assets and subtracting liability
Earning value approach	Evaluate your business based on its ability to continue making wealth in the future
Marketing approach	Estimates your company's value by establishing what your business is worth by the price similar businesses sell for.

Garrett Monroe

Finding Potential Buyers: The Search for the Perfect Match

Finding the right buyer for your business may take time. It involves putting your business up for sale physically or online and searching for the right buyers. **Here are ways to find the perfect buyer that matches your needs:**

- Network with people doing business in your niche, industry professionals, and associations

- Seek buyers online in various online communities and business platforms that can give you a wider audience.

- Hire a business broker, mergers and acquisition advisor, and legal or financial professional experienced in business transactions.

- Explore business broker sites such as Empire Flippers. They specialize in selling a business once it is established.

Negotiating the Sale: Sealing the Deal Gracefully

After you find the perfect buyer, you must enter the negotiating room with an idea of who the buyer is and how much you want from your business. **The steps to follow as you prepare for negotiation are:**

1. Gather information about your business, the current market, the buyer, and the company's projections.

2. Read and practice the negotiation strategies you need to use. Keep in mind your bottom line and other areas that are non-negotiables.

3. Negotiate the selling price by dividing your company into various parts.

4. Prepare the contingencies that must be implemented before completing the sale.

5. Talk to a business advisor to ensure you are making the right decision.

Passing the LLC Baton: Legacy Planning Unveiled

You may not want to sell your business as you retire or go on to another venture. A succession plan is an option to consider to keep your business legacy going. It involves choosing the right person or people to run your company [17]. Let's discuss how to do that.

Estate Planning and Succession: Ensuring Your Vision Lives On

Estate and succession planning brings together the aspect of preparing who will take over your business assets and also the leadership of the company. If you run a single-member LLC, you must transfer ownership and management rights to the next person. However, an LLC with multiple owners permits you to transfer your ownership rights, but the leadership roles must be discussed with all partners. In effecting your plan, you need to have clarity of thought in figuring out what is important to you vs. what is best for the company's future and then striking a balance between the two.

Grooming a Successor: Handing Over the Reins with Care

The successor you choose can take your business to new and better heights or jeopardize your business legacy and run it down. The journey to select a successor starts early, **and the following are the tips you can use as you groom a successor:**

- Identify, interview, and choose a suitable successor who wants to build your company and has the skills to do it.

- Identify and address skills and knowledge gaps the successor may have and work on a plan to rectify them.

- Document essential company processes and ensure they are aware of how things are done.

- Build a strong team that can help the successor achieve the company's goal.

Family Business Considerations: Balancing Blood and Business

Balancing blood and business is a sensitive undertaking because you do not want to appear to be giving special treatment to the family and risk losing trust with the employees or breeding resentment towards the blood successor. You must let your family successor work as hard as the other employees to earn their place as the successor. Using more of the merit instead of the inherit model helps to send a clear message that you are not handing over the company to someone who hasn't met the company's expectations. Even though your family members have a unique position, they must have good performance metrics.

Legal and Tax Implications of Succession: Navigating the Regulatory Maze

Legal or tax implications are a factor you must consider as you work on implementing your succession plan. Whichever approach you choose, you will have to part with some money to meet certain tax requirements. For legal implications, your main task will be updating business licenses, permits, and company documents and transferring contracts and liabilities. Tax implications include capital gain taxes for selling the LLC and gift or estate tax for transferring ownership. To minimize the tax implication, work with a professional who can help you qualify for exemptions and tax breaks.

Closing Down the LLC: A Strategic Farewell

Closing down your LLC ensures you do not accrue financial responsibilities after you've stopped operations. The processes involved notify the various authorities of your decision that all legal processes attached to your LLC should stop. We break down the key things to address as you close down.

Voluntary Dissolution Process: The Final Curtain Call

Voluntary LLC dissolution occurs when members agree to close down the company due to various reasons, such as the death of a member or hard economic times. **The process is as follows:**

1. Have a meeting to dissolve the LLC as per the operating agreement or state laws

2. File the articles of dissolution with your state authorities.

3. File the pending tax returns and pay all debts

4. Take care of pending contracts, sell agreed-upon assets, and distribute the rest

5. Follow any other procedure you included in the operating agreement.

Settling Business Debts and Obligations: Ending on Good Terms

Ending on good terms with your creditors or vendors is a professional and ethical way to handle your pending debts and obligations The creditors might even agree to a lower settlement in an attempt to get some money before you close down [18]. Fortunately, LLCs protect you from creditors seizing your assets, but those same creditors can come for your company's assets as a way to get a portion of their money. Try to work things out with them, as they have helped you keep your business doors open.

Distributing Assets to Members: Wrapping Up the Finances

Legally, distributing assets to members should not take place until you have settled all the debts with creditors. Afterward, the members can divide the assets according to the provisions outlined in the operating agreement. **Take the following steps to distribute assets fairly:**

1. Sell tangible assets for cash

2. Share out the gain or loss realized from the sale to partners (as per the income rations)

3. Pay liabilities in cash to the partners

4. Distribute the remaining cash on the basis of capital balances.

Filing Final Tax Returns and Compliance: The Last Chapter in LLC Life

As you close your LLC, one of the last vital steps is to file your final tax return and close all tax accounts with the IRS and state. If you have a payroll or sales tax account, ensure it is funded correctly and up to date. To close your IRS tax account, you must file a final Form 1065 if you run a multi-member LLC and Form 1040 for a single-member LLC. Ensure you check the final return box. The other members should also tick the final return box in their Schedule-K-1 form before transferring the income or loss to their personal tax return form. Finally, confirm with your local, county, and state authorities that you have complied with all the guidelines in closing an LLC.

Key Takeaways

- When planning to sell your LLC, you must assess the buyers' needs and meet those standards to optimize your company's value.

- Using more of the merit instead of the inherit model helps to send a clear message that you are not handing over the company to a family member who hasn't met the company's expectations.

- Closing down your LLC officially with various authorities ensures you stop accruing financial responsibilities when you cease operations.

Chapter 9

Unveiling Triumphs: LLC Case Studies

> "Success isn't about what you accomplish in life; it's about what you inspire others to do."
>
> **-Anonymous**

Industry Insights: Profiling Successful LLCs

As mentioned in earlier chapters, LLCs are the most favorable business structure for entrepreneurs starting a business. This section will share two stories of people who chose to form an LLC from the onset and how it worked out for them. Afterward, we will see the valuable insights you can gain from them and others.

Diverse Tales of LLC Triumphs

Our first story is that of Zach Ranen, founder of RAIZE bakery. He discovered a niche that enabled him to reinvent traditional cookies and modernize them to meet the current market trends. He researched the various business structures and chose to form an LLC. Zach did not want the cumbersome paperwork of a corporation but still wanted to protect his personal assets from liability when he expanded. He worked with a company that assists new entrepreneurs in forming LLCs and was advised to register his LLC in Delaware and qualify the LLC in New York state. Within a short period, he was up and running as an LLC in New York.

Our second story is that of Brian Chesky and Joe Gebbia, the founders of Airbnb. They were undergoing financial challenges and decided to transform their apartment in San Francisco into a rental space. What started as a simple solution to their problem became a major online platform where people could make money by renting their spaces, and others would find affordable places to stay as they travel. Although it currently operates as a publicly traded company, its initial business structure was similar to that of an LLC.

Airbnb hosts often utilize the asset protection of LLC formations when operating their business. Establishing an LLC protects your personal finances and assets from financial penalties or legal actions that might result from hosting an Airbnb property.

Gaining Valuable Insights from Real-Life Stories

The above two stories and other success stories from famous LLC companies like Google LLC, Blackberry LLC, and eBay LLC have helped rising entrepreneurs gain insights into running their own LLCs [19]. **These valuable insights include:**

- Beginning small and keeping costs down to avoid depending heavily on outside funding.

- Understanding your area of expertise and narrowing it down until you find your unique selling point.

- Realizing when it's time to bring in an expert to help you set up your LLC to ensure you take care of all the legal and tax requirements.

- Knowing when to formalize the LLC to make sure you benefit from the tax benefits and personal asset protection.

- Calculate when you should pay yourself vs. put back the profits into the business to enable further growth.

- Realizing when it's time to change to another business structure to allow scaling into greater heights.

- Understanding the need to form meaningful work associations and create a warm, caring relationship with the customers.

Strategic Moves: Navigating Success

You will rarely find a successful LLC that does not have to apply particular strategies to get to the high-achieving level it operates on. For instance, they had to stop some activities and learn new ones. These success strategies required them to stay up-to-date with emerging trends and study their company's operational methods. Let's learn some of these strategies and discover other lessons picked by the pros.

Vital Strategies and Decision-Making That Paved the Way

As you have learned in the earlier chapters, having a business idea and the passion to start a business is not enough. You must think about, and research vital strategies to implement that pave the way for success. **The following are strategies and decisions successful LLC owners had to consider in order to succeed:**

- They clearly defined their niche, found their target market, and put all efforts into winning their ideal customers.

- They started with as little expenses as possible and minimized upfront fees while taking advantage of the available free or inexpensive resources.

- They accepted that technology is here to stay and found a way to use it to their advantage while adding a human touch where possible.

- They closely monitored their financial records, ensuring they remained disciplined and had significant cash reserves to address unavoidable crises.

- They made it their goal to establish a healthy company culture that addressed the employees' and customers' needs and held them in high esteem.

- They created systems to assist them in addressing arising challenges and take advantage of the flexibility LLCs offer.

Lessons Learned from the Pros

Let's learn directly from some of the famous people who started successful businesses and what their most important lessons are:

1. "Focus narrowly on excelling in one core competency vs trying to be everything to everyone." - Linda Findley Kozlowski, founder of Etsy (handmade goods marketplace)

2. "Obsess over the problems you are solving for your customers - not external validation or vanity metrics," said Katia Beauchamp, co-founder of Birchbox (beauty product sampling).

3. "Company culture and shared values define and unite a business - make them a priority starting day one." - Christine Tao, founder of Sounding Board (business coaching).

4. "Obsess over customer experience and satisfaction - negative word of mouth can tank a small business." - Tristan Walker, founder of Walker & Company Brands (health and beauty products)

5. "Be frugal and bootstrap as much as possible in the early days to preserve control and flexibility," said Tobi Lütke, founder of Shopify (e-commerce platform).

6. "Focus on building a product or service that delivers outstanding value," said Sahil Lavingia, founder of Gumroad (e-commerce platform).

7. "Pay close attention to cash flow and financing from day one, managing budgets rigorously even during growth stages." - Jenn Hyman, founder of Rent the Runway (designer dress rental).

Overcoming Obstacles: LLC Challenges Conquered

As business owners, we have faced various challenges as we ran our businesses. We have also helped countless entrepreneurs overcome obstacles they have experienced as they began their businesses and in the growth process. Here is what we have to say about overcoming obstacles.

The Grit and Determination Behind Success

Grit is a quality most entrepreneurs should have because it helps you to keep going when things get tough. It propels you forward to achieve your business goals even when the outlook seems bleak. Entrepreneurs with grit motivate themselves to move forward. They do not view failure as the end but see it as a business approach that doesn't work [20]. It sets them forth to look for another strategy with the lesson they learned from the failure in mind. **Ways to enhance your grit are:**

- Improve your performance by setting goals and assessing your progress often.

- Focus on your passion and purpose when facing hardships.

- Accept failure and move on without beating yourself down.

- Develop attainable goals and be realistic about the outcomes desired.

- From a team to lean on when challenges come.

- Manage your emotions. Never get too high after the wins or too low after the losses. Stay even keel, and consistently move forward as you chart your path to success.

A Deeper Dive into Triumph Over Troubles

When going through changes in your LLC, you may feel like the troubles are too much, and you cannot see a way out or a sign of triumph on the horizon. You probably know there's nothing new under the sun, meaning countless entrepreneurs have gone through the troubles you are going through now. What set apart those who triumphed and those who remained in their troubles was their mindset. The following table compares the mindset of people who triumph sooner vs. those who stay in business troubles longer.

	Triumph Mindset	Trouble Mindset
Attitude	Optimistic and confident	Pessimistic and threatened
Planning	Strategic and adaptable	Rigid and stressed
Finances	Stabilizes reserves and controls costs	Erratic spending cuts

Resilience	Leverage challenges to get better	Demoralized by challenges
Focus	Sees opportunity	Sees obstacles

Learning from Legends: Key Takeaways

In this chapter, we have learned various insights and lessons from successful LLC owners. This section will address the key takeaways you can pick from the diverse insights learned by the legends and throughout this guidebook.

Extracting Nuggets of Wisdom

Nuggets of wisdom often come from people who have gone through an arduous journey, emerged on the other side, and lived to tell the tale (and have a few tips to improve that journey, too!). In business, these nuggets of wisdom can affect the company directly or indirectly. **The following are nuggets we have lived by as entrepreneurs and still aim at making them our regular practice:**

- Step out of your comfort zone and take more risks. You'll be surprised by the new experiences you will encounter.

- Eat well, exercise, and get enough sleep. Depriving yourself using unhealthy practices limits the mental and physical capacity you bring to the business.

- Be quick to appreciate and encourage your team for their outstanding work. It creates more loyalty and commitment to the company.

- Recognize high performance and nurture its growth while eliminating underperformance by addressing the points of weakness.

- If you think a task, idea, or challenge is hard, adjust your mindset, and you'll be surprised how your approach changes.

- Think through any business advice you receive; do not ignore your intuition and your personal experiences.

Applying Battle-Tested Best Practices to Your LLC

As the LLC leader, you assume all responsibility for your company's performance. Therefore, it is important to identify the best business practices for smooth operation, compliance, and a positive relationship between partners, employees, and clients. **Here are some critical battle-tested practices to implement:**

- Understand the basics of an LLC and implement the essential aspects

- Develop an operating agreement and use it as a reference for disputes

- Keep good and accurate financial records

- Comply with crucial state and federal-specific requirements

- Protect your LLC with favorable insurance coverage

- Take advantage of tax benefits and stay compliant

- Adapt to emerging changes and consider scaling upwards

Sidestepping Common Pitfalls with Confidence

Becoming a successful business owner is rewarding. But you must put in the hard work and avoid common pitfalls that may cause you to stagnate or close down your company. The following table shows the common pitfalls you may encounter and how to sidestep them.

Common Pitfall	How to Sidestep with Confidence
Forming LLC in the wrong state	Form the LLC in the state in which you plan to conduct business if you want to avoid DBA issues
Failing to separate personal and business finances	Form the LLC in the state in which you plan to conduct business if you want to avoid DBA issues
Having a weak operating agreement	Draft a detailed and dependable operating agreement to cater to arising LLC matters
Not consulting professionals	Talk to diverse professionals experienced in crucial areas in your LLC to help you cover all legal, financial, and tax grounds

From the onset, aim to build a strong foundation for your LLC business by avoiding these common pitfalls so that you can withstand any storms that may come your way.

Key Takeaways

- A key industry insight is to begin in a small way and keep costs down to avoid depending heavily on outside funding.

- Having a business idea and the passion to start a business is not enough. You must research vital strategies implemented by successful LLC owners and do the same or improve on them.

- Entrepreneurs with grit motivate themselves to move forward and learn from mistakes as they grow.

- Applying best business practices ensures your operations run smoothly, remain compliant, and have a healthy relationship with your partners, employees, and customers.

Chapter 10

Key Resources

Legal and Business Resources

This section focuses on giving you the necessary resources to assist you in kickstarting your LLC. We shall provide helpful legal and government resources and explain how to establish a virtual office.

Online Legal Resources

- LLC (Limited Liability Company) - Start an LLC | LegalZoom: https://bit.ly/LegalZoomLLCGuide

- LLC Laws by State - LLC Statutes by State: https://howtostartanllc.com/llc-statute

- 50-State Guide to Forming an LLC | Nolo: https://bit.ly/50stateLLC

- LLC Annual Fees by State - All 50 States [2023 Costs] | LLCU®: https://bit.ly/LLCbyState

- URS Agents | Registered Agent Services:

https://bit.ly/LLCRegisteredAgent

- All 50 State Agencies That Issue Small Business Licenses and Permits: https://bit.ly/SmallBizLicense

- Best Small-Business Insurance 2023: Compare Options - NerdWallet: https://bit.ly/LLCSmallBizInsurance

Government Websites and Agencies

- Stay legally compliant | U.S. Small Business Administration: https://bit.ly/LegalComplianceLLC

- Apply for licenses and permits | U.S. Small Business Administration: https://bit.ly/LicenseAndPermitsLLC

- Your account | Internal Revenue Service (irs.gov): https://www.irs.gov/your-account

- New and Small Businesses | U.S. Department of Labor: https://bit.ly/DolLLC

- Apply for an Employer Identification Number (EIN) Online | Internal Revenue Service: https://bit.ly/EinAppLLC

- Trademarks | USPTO: Trademarks | USPTO:

Legal Forms and Templates

- 2022 Form 1040: https://www.irs.gov/pub/irs-pdf/f1040.pdf

- 2023 Form 1040-ES: https://www.irs.gov/pub/irs-pdf/f1040es.pdf

- 2023 Schedule C (Form 1040): https://www.irs.gov/pub/irs-pdf/f1040sc.pdf

- 2022 Schedule K-1 (Form 1041): https://www.irs.gov/pub/irs-pdf/f1041sk1.pdf

- 2022 Form 1065: https://www.irs.gov/pub/irs-pdf/f1065.pdf

- Free Business Plan Template with Examples (PDF): https://www.lawdistrict.com/business-plan/

- Free LLC Operating Agreement Template (US): https://www.lawdistrict.com/llc-operating-agreement/

- Free Multi-Member LLC Operating Agreement: https://www.lawdistrict.com/llc-operating-agreement/multi-member/

- Single Member LLC Operating Agreement - PDF: https://www.lawdistrict.com/llc-operating-agreement/single-member/

Setting up a virtual office/phone number for your LLC

As you start your LLC, you'll need a mailing address to include in your company's formation documents and a place to receive mail. If you don't have a commercial office space, you can use a PO Box or home address, but this is not the safest method. Besides, some states and local areas do not permit PO Box use. You can solve this challenge by acquiring a virtual address.

A virtual address allows you to use an actual street address as your company's virtual mailbox. This enables you to receive all important mail and protect your privacy. It also gives your business a professional image, as the mail center is usually in a commercial area. Most virtual offices also have phone numbers they can assign to your LLC and registered agents for receiving your documents. It's usually possible to set up mail forwarding to your home address as well.

Online Tools and Software

Starting a business in this day and age allows you to take advantage of advanced technology. You can automate various tasks and use software that limits human errors. Consider setting up the following tools in your LLC.

Accounting and Bookkeeping Tools

- Expensify | Spend Management Software for Receipts & Expenses: https://www.expensify.com/

- TurboTax® Official Site: File Taxes Online, Tax Filing Made Easy: https://turbotax.intuit.com/

- Simple Double-Entry Accounting For Your Business - FreshBooks: https://bit.ly/freshbooksLLC

- Best Online Accounting Software for your business in USA - Zoho Books: https://www.zoho.com/us/books/

- Oracle NetSuite: https://bit.ly/OracleForLLC

- Free Cloud Accounting Software | Odoo: https://bit.ly/OdooLLC

Project Management Software

- Zapier | Automation that moves you forward: https://zapier.com/

- Manage your team's work, projects, & tasks online • Asana: https://asana.com/

- Google Workspace: Secure Online Productivity & Collaboration Tools: https://workspace.google.com/

- Xodo Sign Free Trial (eversign.com): https://eversign.com/trial/docracy

- Where work happens | Slack: https://slack.com/

Marketing and SEO Tools

- Canva: Visual Suite for Everyone: https://www.canva.com/

- Kickstarter: https://www.kickstarter.com/

- Social Media Marketing and Management Tool: https://www.hootsuite.com/

- Analytics Tools & Solutions for Your Business - Google Analytics: https://marketingplatform.google.com/about/analytics/

- Free Tools | HubSpot: https://www.hubspot.com

- Marketing, Automation & Email Platform | Mailchimp: https://mailchimp.com/

Communication and Collaboration Tools

- OpenPhone | Modern business phone for startups and small businesses: https://www.openphone.com/

- 10 BEST Virtual Address for Business & Mailbox Services (2023): https://www.guru99.com/best-virtual-mailbox-service.html

- Collaboration Tools and Solutions for Business | Teams: https://www.microsoft.com/en-us/microsoft-teams/collaboration

- Online Whiteboard for Team Collaboration | Miro: https://bit.ly/LLCCollab

- Confluence - Team Collaboration Software | Atlassian: https://bit.ly/AtLassLLC

Internalizing the Entrepreneurial Mindset

Before we wrap up here, we're going to give you a few mindset-oriented tips that every entrepreneur should know.

Starting and growing a business is a journey. There will be ups and downs, and your ability to navigate those with a clear head will determine whether or not you succeed in the long run.

So as you embark on this journey, remember the following:

Even Keel is the Way to Go

You'll have a myriad of wins and losses as an entrepreneur. The key is to not get too high during the wins, or too low during the losses. The better you can manage your emotions through the ups and downs, the more consistently you'll perform, and the better off your business will be.

Of course, this is easier said than done.

Here's a few tips on managing your emotions:

- Make sure you sleep 7-8 hours every night, in a dark cold room.

- Whenever you feel stressed, take a few minutes and focus on your breath. Breathe deeply, count to five on the inhale, exhale, and hold in between. This will calm you down and ground you.

- Eat healthy. Your mental state is a reflection of what you consume and put into your body. If that's a ton of processed junk food, you'll find it exceedingly hard to feel good and manage your emotions. On the other hand, if you eat clean and healthy and limit the junk food, you'll have more clarity and a better emotional baseline.

- Take time off. We recommend taking at least one day off each week where you do nothing business-related. This will help you reset, unwind, and mentally prepare yourself for the week of work. It'll also help you avoid bouts of burnout, which can set you back weeks.

- Have a fitness routine. Whether it be walking, hitting the gym, or playing a sport - moving your body consistently is great for mental health.

- Limit alcohol consumption. There's no way around it - when you push your limits in business, you often operate at your edge.

Drinking, even a little bit, can tip you over that edge and set you back in a big way. Especially during periods of intense work, it's a good idea to limit alcohol intake.

Contribution Breaks the Curse

We've had a few lows on our business journey. For example, early on in a coaching business of ours, we hit a rough month of sales, where after averaging $50-100k in revenue monthly, there was a dry patch with no sales for a three-week span.

It was one of those periods where it felt like we'd never see a sale roll in again. Coaching applications were drying up, hardly anyone was scheduling calls, and it felt like our leads were more unqualified than ever.

Instead of going down with the ship and freaking out, we decided to take massive action. We hit the pavement and started making tons of lead-generating content on YouTube, Instagram, and TikTok.

Within a few weeks, the curse was indeed broken. We managed to hit $50k in sales that month, and followed it up with a record-breaking month the following month.

Taking action will make you feel better, and as a result you'll show up to clients and prospects better. Additionally, it'll set the stage to bring in more leads and create more business in the short and long term.

Offense vs Defense

Most people live their lives perpetually on defense. They take very few risks, and as a result, don't typically reap big rewards.

But if you want to build a thriving business, you've got to get used to playing offense. Sure, there's a time and place for defense and being in "protection mode." But if you don't play offense and shift into an "attack mode" mentality, you won't have much to protect in the first place.

Have a Solution-Focused Approach

With a solution-focused approach, you focus on solving the problems that come up, rather than being hyper-focused on the problems themselves (and having a freak-out, like many people do).

This allows you to stay calm, cool, and collected, and generate solutions that help you to maintain and grow your business.

If you want help building a rock-solid mindset, we show you exactly how to do it in our "10 Mindfulness Hacks for Entrepreneurs" PDF included in the free 7-Figure Business Toolkit. You can download it here: llclegend.com/llc-s-corp-bonus.

Conclusion

An LLC is one of the best structures to choose as you start your business journey. Even though it has vital legal and financial implications, the benefits outweigh the responsibilities. The process may appear complicated and even scary in the beginning. However, this guidebook has given you the core requirements and best practices for properly setting up and running an LLC.

At this point, you have probably figured out why it would be best to choose an LLC instead of some other legal entity, such as a greater level of personal liability protection and taxation flexibility. In addition, you got a step-by-step guide on the formation process, including selecting a company name, hiring a registered agent to file your articles of organization, and drafting an operating agreement. You also learned of the ongoing maintenance requirements, such as holding members' meetings, submitting annual reports, and staying compliant.

Even though every state has its own LLC regulations, this guidebook has outlined general aspects that all LLC founders in whichever state can apply. If you use the information provided within every page of this book, you will have the ability to fulfill all federal, state, and local obligations, as well as open business accounts, obtain an EIN, and purchase necessary insurance policies.

You also have the legal and government resources you need to start working on your LLC at your disposal. Not only that, but we have also outlined marketing, accounting, and project management tools that will assist you in performing some tasks from the onset, which will help you streamline everything.

Along the way, you might face the complex legal situations involved in scaling your business, bringing additional investors, mergers and acquisitions, or expanding beyond the state limits. When that time comes, you should talk with business lawyers and financial advisors as you work on amending your operating agreements. Even at this point, this guidebook has provided you with reliable information that can help you know what action to take.

But for now, you are armed with the knowledge you need to start your LLC confidently. The administrative duties may seem cumbersome, but you understand exactly what it takes to comply. The most important thing is that your business has proper legal support and structure that makes it possible for you to develop a successful, profitable business in due time.

Starting an LLC is the road less traveled, and it has its ups and downs, but remember, your dreams are worth the investment of time and resources. Remain committed to your vision, but be flexible along the way. Surround yourself with people who share your aspiration to build a successful business. There will be trials, yet it is these challenges that propel you forward when you overcome them. What lies behind doesn't compare to the bold future you are building. You are strong; therefore, dream big and allow the inside adventurer in you to come alive. Congratulations on taking these important first steps, and best of luck executing your vision within a stable, smart LLC entity designed for long-term growth.

References

1. Corporation Requirements: Everything You Need to Know. (n.d.). UpCounsel. https://www.upcounsel.com/corporation-requirements#:~:text=These%20continuous%20requirements%20include%20those%20related%20to%20the, . . .%206%20State%20registration. %20. . .%207%20Licensing. %20

2. What is an operating agreement? Do I need one for my LLC? (2023, November 9). Thomson Reuters Legal. https://legal.thomsonreuters.com/en/insights/articles/what-is-an-operating-agreement

3. Tarver, E. (2023, November 1). Market segmentation: definition, example, types, benefits. Investopedia. https://www.investopedia.com/terms/m/marketsegmentation.asp

4. Business compliance requirements & consequences. (2021, January 26). https://www.wolterskluwer.com/en/expert-insights/business-compliance-requirements-and-consequences

5. Having an LLC in multiple states. (n.d.). https://formationscorp.com/blog/having-an-llc-in-multiple-states

6. How to apply for an EIN | Internal Revenue Service. (n.d.). https://www.irs.gov/businesses/small-businesses-self-employed/how-to-apply-for-an-ein

7. Staff, C. (2023, December 1). Conflict Management: Definition, Strategies, and Styles. Coursera. https://www.coursera.org/articles/conflict-management

8. Apply for licenses and permits. (n.d.). U.S. Small Business Administration. https://www.sba.gov/business-guide/launch-your-business/apply-licenses-permits

9. McCullah, S. (2022b, April 4). Debt financing vs. equity financing: Do you want to take out a loan or take on investors? Business Insider. https://www.businessinsider.com/personal-finance/debt-financing-vs-equity-financing

10. 4 Examples of business negotiation Strategies | HBS Online. (2023, June 15). Business Insights Blog. https://online.hbs.edu/blog/post/negotiating-in-business

11. Collaboration and Partnership: How to build strong alliances for business success. (n.d.). https://www.strategicadvisorboard.com/blog-posts/collaboration-and-partnership-how-to-build-strong-alliances-for-business-success#:~:text=Steps%20to%20Building%20Strong%20Alliances%201%201.%20Define,communication%20plan%20. . .%206%206.%20Manage%20the%20partnership

12. Robinson, A. (2022, November 30). 14 Crucial HR skills, Competencies & qualifications. teambuilding.com. https://teambuilding.com/blog/hr-skills

13. Abhi, T. P. (2023, December 13). Brand Protection 101: Ensuring the security of your brand online. Promote Abhi. https://www.promoteabhi.com/blog/brand-protection-guide

14. Indeed Editorial Team. "10 Types of Business Risks and How to Manage Them." Indeed Career Guide, www.indeed.com/career-advice/starting-new-job/types-of-business-risk

15. 5 Common Misconceptions about the R&D Tax Credit—and Whether You Qualify. (2021, March 12). https://www.mossadams.com/articles/2021/03/company-qualifications-for-the-r-d-tax-credit

16. eMoney Advisor. (2023, December 7). Creating a Financial Advisor Business Plan: A Comprehensive guide. https://emoneyadvisor.com/blog/creating-a-financial-advisor-business-plan-a-comprehensive-guide/

17. deloitteeditor. (2021, March 13). Leaving a legacy for your company, your team, and yourself. WSJ. https://deloitte.wsj.com/cfo/leaving-a-legacy-for-your-company-your-team-and-yourself-01552435330

18. Feldman, S. (2024, July 31). How to close an LLC: Dissolution, winding up, and termination. https://www.wolterskluwer.com/en/expert-insights/dissolving-winding-up-and-terminating-a-limited-liability-company?

19. Petersen, R. (2021, June 19). 15 inspiring case studies of pivoting. BarnRaisers, LLC. https://barnraisersllc.com/2021/06/19/15-inspiring-case-studies-of-pivoting/

20. Todd, D. (2021, December 30). Passion, grit, resilience: the formula for success. Entrepreneur. https://www.entrepreneur.com/leadership/passion-grit-resilience-the-formula-for-success/

Book 2

The Only S Corporation Beginner's Guide You'll Ever Need

A Roadmap on Starting & Managing Your S Corp
(Plus, Bookkeeping & Accounting Tips to Reduce
Small Business Taxes)

By

Garrett Monroe

The Only S Corp Beginner's Guide You'll Ever Need

You've got a dream to start your own business, or maybe even turn it into a thriving enterprise.

Perhaps you're fired up with aspirations that your vision will change the world, like Apple or Tesla.

Or maybe you just want to create more freedom and build a fantastic and lucrative lifestyle for yourself. Whatever your lofty (but attainable) ambitions, before anything else, you need to make sure you've protected yourself from the liabilities such an undertaking entails in order to set yourself up for success. Selecting the right business framework is so very crucial. In this book, we'll tackle the concept and benefits of one of the most preferred structures—the S corporation.

Picture this ideal set-up: a business framework that effortlessly combines corporate liability protection with the tax advantages of a partnership. That's exactly what an S corporation does—it gives you a powerful strategy to safeguard personal assets and maximize tax benefits. It goes beyond just the legal framework; it's a dynamic and strategic tool for navigating business intricacies. With the appropriate structure, you can navigate challenges, leverage market changes, and ensure lasting growth so that your business not only survives but also thrives.

The S corporation shields you from personal liability, but it also opens doors to tax savings, enabling reinvestment for growth. It becomes a strategic asset, aligning with your long-term goals and enhancing operational agility.

Imagine attracting top talent through employee-friendly benefits that position your enterprise as a strong industry player. The S corporation is more than just a decision—it's an unbelievably powerful advantage.

Throughout this book, we'll unravel the intricacies of S corporations, equipping you with the knowledge to make informed decisions. From the basics distinguishing S corporations to advanced strategies for business success, this comprehensive but accessible guide will serve as your compass in navigating corporate structures.

Whether you're a seasoned entrepreneur reassessing your business structure or a new visionary seeking a startup foundation, you'll embark with us on a fascinating journey through the realm of S corporations. What's more, you'll discover how this adaptable entity can propel your business to unprecedented success, turning your dreams into reality.

Navigating business structures can be a daunting process; after all, choosing the right one is essential. If you're contemplating whether an S corporation is the optimal choice for your business, you've made a great decision by picking up this book.

The Only S Corporation Beginners Guide You'll Ever Need explains complex topics in simple terms. **Here's what you'll learn:**

- The ins and outs of an S corporation, including why businesses choose an S corporation over an LLC or a C corporation

- Step-by-step instructions on how to set up your S corporation,

- from selecting your business name to drafting corporate bylaws and financing your vision

- How to craft your S corporation tax strategy to save on personal taxes and unlock S corporation tax credits

- How to navigate the intricacies of finance and make the S corporation work for you

- How to set up and understand bookkeeping principles, and when to hire an accountant to help

- Crucial information about taxation, recordkeeping, and operating agreements

- Strategies to minimize taxes using proper deductions and credits

- How to hire talent, set up and oversee payroll, manage and motivate employees, and build a loyal workforce

- How to ensure compliance with all federal and state regulations concerning health and safety standards, environmental regulations, and ethical concerns

- Strategies for expanding your business while upholding your vision and mission

- Factors to consider when selling your business or transitioning it to a successor

You can be sure that this information is factual, reliable, and drawn from experience. Under the pen name Garrett Monroe, this book was created by a team of writers with varied business experience from multiple industries—including sales, AI, real estate, coaching, and accounting. We've pooled our extensive experience to assist you in achieving success in your business venture. We'll demystify the clutter surrounding S corporations, dispel some common myths while informing you of the realities, and set you up on a track to go forth with this advantageous business concept.

Setting up a business structure shouldn't cause you to lose sleep or be riddled with worry. Instead of closing your eyes and blindly choosing a structure you "hope" will work for you in the future, The Only S Corporation Beginners Guide You'll Ever Need will walk you step-by-step through the process. Think of us as your trusted advisors who are helping you set up a blueprint for progress and profit.

We'll start with the basics and introduce you to the tips and strategies we've discovered while setting up and working with other S corporations. But we'll also go far beyond that. You'll be guided through all aspects of running an S Corporation—from bookkeeping and employee payroll to leaving a legacy for your heirs. By the end of this book, you'll feel confident in your choice of business structure and have a solid framework going forward. That way, you can get back to what you do best—creating and selling your product or service.

Chapter 1

Demystifying S Corporations: A Tactical Guide

"The secret of getting ahead is getting started. The secret to getting started is breaking your complex overwhelming tasks into small manageable tasks, and then starting on the first one."
-Mark Twain, American author

Simply put, an S corporation is a legal framework that outlines the organization and taxation structure of your business. Certain guidelines must be adhered to during the incorporation setup, and specific steps need to be followed throughout the year. In this chapter, we'll introduce you to S corporations and why people choose them (hint: it has a lot to do with taxes). We'll also delve into drawbacks to the structure; why you may want to choose an S Corporation versus an LLC, sole proprietorship, partnership, or C corporation; and the basic organizational structure that is required.

The S Corporation Explained: A Primer

An S corporation's biggest advantage is that it can avoid paying corporate taxes. While corporations in a broader sense have been around since the early 1800s, S corporations were created by Congress in 1958 as a way to avoid double taxation. The structure also served to bridge a gap between sole proprietors or partnerships and big corporations. S corporations have opened the doors for entrepreneurship, providing smaller businesses with an opportunity to compete in the saturated marketplace. Today, over 4.5 million US companies use the S corporation structure.

The Essentials of S Corporation Status

In order to be recognized as an S corporation, a company must adhere to the stipulations outlined in Chapter 1, **Subchapter S of the Internal Revenue Code.[1] They must:**

- Have their headquarters situated in the United States

- Have 100 or fewer shareholders that satisfy specific conditions

- Authorize and issue only one category of stock

- Meet eligibility requirements (the S corporation structure may not be utilized by certain financial institutions, insurance firms, and domestic international sales corporations)

The Edge of Pass-Through Taxation

One of the primary benefits of an S corporation is how taxes are assessed. Regular corporations are taxed twice on the same income— once at the corporate level (where they pay taxes on annual earnings) and once at the individual level (where the shareholders pay taxes on the dividends they receive with a K-1 and a W-2 from salaries). An S corporation doesn't incur taxes on its earnings but rather passes the income, loss, credits, and deductions to the shareholders. The shareholders then report these items on their personal tax returns through salaries and dividends.

There are exceptions to this rule. For example, if your corporation is located in certain municipalities or states (New York City or California, for example), you may be subject to taxes that mimic the corporate tax. We'll cover more on this topic later in the book.

The Drawbacks: Understanding the Limitations

Prior to reaching a decision, it's crucial to grasp every facet of an S corporation, encompassing all of its limitations and potential drawbacks.

First, S corporations require more protocols, including the required board of directors and shareholder meetings, meeting minutes, formal bylaws, and strict recordkeeping requirements. Bookkeeping and accounting are more complex, and many business owners choose to hire professionals to keep up with the myriad of fees and taxes.

Second, the IRS keeps a close eye on S corporations to ensure that shareholders aren't reporting low salaries and high dividends to lower their tax burden. Distributions must be allocated on the number of shares or percentage of ownership of each shareholder. The IRS won't hesitate to revoke an S corporation's status for non-compliance reasons. Fortunately, however, the IRS typically remits you to rectify the situation.

Third, S corporation setup and compliance can be pricey when submitting proper fees and documents. An S corporation must have a registered agent, and you'll most likely be hiring someone to keep up with the requirements.

Finally, because S corporations have limitations on the number and residential status of shareholders and stock classes, a fast-growing company's expansion and success might be restricted.

Business Structure Battlefield: S Corp vs. The Rest

Let's take a few minutes to compare S corporations with the two other popular legal entities—LLCs and C corporations.

LLCs

S corporations afford the same limited liability as an LLC. They're both pass-through entities that are exempt from corporate taxes, and both afford protection from lawsuits and business creditors. In addition, both entities can leverage tax benefits provided by the Tax Cuts and Jobs Act.

S corporations, specifically, enjoy a distinct advantage in the realm of self-employment taxes. With an LLC, these taxes are imposed on the company's entire net business income. But with an S corporation, the shareholder receives a salary (which is charged self-employment tax) and dividends (which isn't charged self-employment tax). The result? In most cases, significant tax savings.

An S corporation also has an advantage when it comes to longevity, as it's easy to transfer ownership. With an LLC, sole proprietorship, or partnership, the entire organization is potentially in jeopardy if one of the principal owners decides to depart the company.

If you get to the point where you need to expand and wish to obtain financing from outside vendors or private equity funds, you'll likely need to convert to a C corporation. At that point, S corporations simply need to file a form with the IRS, while LLCs will essentially need a complete restructuring that takes time and money, two things that you're likely not willing to part with.

An LLC, however, does offer more flexibility. It can distribute profits and losses without strict IRS regulations, and it isn't subject to strict guidelines and reporting requirements.

C Corporations

We've already mentioned the double taxation issue with C corporations, which is one of the main reasons to choose an S corporation instead. But let's dive a little further into this type of structure.

One of the biggest advantages of C corporations is that they offer more growth opportunities. They can have unlimited shareholders and different classes of stock, and they can be located anywhere in the world. Fast-growing companies might want to hop directly to C corporation status to avoid the hassle of conversion when they choose to expand. On the other hand, some companies form an S corporation for the first few years of their existence to take advantage of the tax savings while they grow their business.

Success in Action: Spotlight on S Corporation Achievers

Reality check: Choosing an S corporation doesn't necessarily guarantee success. As with any undertaking, starting a business requires extensive planning and unwavering dedication. That said, there are some key factors that can definitely contribute to the success of an S corporation. **They include:**

- **A Clear Business Strategy:** Outline the company's mission, vision, goals, and strategies to more easily achieve them. Adapt your approach to align with the fluctuations in marketing conditions.

- **A Strong Leadership Team:** Choose leaders who can make informed decisions, motivate employees, and navigate the challenges of the business environment.

- **Sound Financial Practices:** Prioritize budgeting, oversee cash flow, control expenses, and execute strategic financial decisions.

- **Exceptional Customer Service:** Cultivate positive connections with customers to nurture loyalty and promote repeat business.

- **Embracing Innovation:** Leverage technology to enhance efficiency, productivity, and customer experiences.

- **Cultivating a Talented and Motivated Workforce:** Invest in employee training, provide opportunities for professional development, and foster a positive work culture.

- **Adherence to Laws and Regulations:** Comply with federal, state, and local regulations regarding taxes, industry-specific rules, and ethical business practices.

- **Risk Management:** Have contingency plans, insurance coverage, and strategies in place to mitigate potential internal and external risks.

- **Strategic Tax Planning:** Take advantage of available deductions, credits, and incentives.

Top Reasons for Selecting an S Corporation

1. This will be mentioned often, but the main benefit of selecting an S corporation is the tax structure.

2. The personal assets of shareholders in an S corporation are safeguarded, with no obligation for shareholders to assume the business' liabilities and debts.

3. An S corporation isn't dependent on shareholders staying with the company. If a shareholder decides to exit the business or you decide to sell the company, it's relatively easy to transfer interest.

4. Creating an S corporation elevates your business' credibility. Suppliers, clients, investors, and collaborators appreciate the corporate designation.

Financial Frontiers: Taxes and S Corporations

Let's take a deeper dive into the tax structure of an S corporation. After all, you want to reduce your tax burden as much as possible, and S corporations offer a fantastic opportunity to do this.

Navigating Tax Benefits and Implications

In addition to pass-through taxation and avoidance of double taxation, **below are a few other tax benefits for S corporations:**

- Shareholders may be eligible for the QBI (Qualified Business Income) deduction, which allows them to deduct up to 20% of qualified business income (such as capital gains and losses, dividends, and interest income) on their personal tax return.

- Shareholders who are also employees may receive tax-favored fringe benefits (such as health insurance, retirement plan contributions, and other employee benefits). These can be deducted as business expenses on tax returns.

- Shareholders have the ability to deduct their allocated S corporation losses on their individual tax returns, thereby mitigating income from alternative sources.

- Shareholders receive profit distributions according to their percentage of ownership in the company.

- When S corporation assets are sold, shareholders may be eligible for capital gains treatment on their share of the proceeds, which can result in lower tax rates.

On the other end of the spectrum, S corporations can be faced with the following tax implications:

- If a C corporation changes to an S corporation status and sells appreciated assets in a certain time period, the corporation may be subject to a built-in gains tax.

- Taxes may be higher if an S corporation has significant passive income (such as dividends, interest, or rental income).

- Shareholders who serve as employees must receive a fair salary for their provided services, and the S corporation is required to cover relevant payroll taxes.

- An S corporation has a limit of 100 shareholders, and they must satisfy specific criteria.

- Shareholders can only deduct S corporation losses up to the amount of their share of the company. If the losses exceed that amount, they must be carried forward.

- S corporations must comply with the regulations of the state in which they're incorporated and conduct business.

Asset Armor: Liability Protection Explored

An S corporation is an attractive choice for many business owners due to its limitations on liability. Due to its status as a distinct legal entity from its shareholders, the personal assets of individual shareholders are shielded in the case of an S corporation. In the event that the business faces financial difficulties or legal issues, creditors cannot pursue shareholders' personal assets to satisfy business debts.

This liability also extends to contractual obligations. When the S corporation enters into contracts or agreements, the entity is legally responsible—not individual shareholders.

Shareholders are, however, personally liable for certain actions, such as personal guarantees, intentional misconduct, or illegal activities. Nevertheless, the action of one shareholder does not typically carry over to other shareholders.

Additional assurances that protect shareholders from liability include maintaining corporate protocols as well as a clear separation between personal and business finances. General liability insurance, professional liability insurance, and other forms of coverage will also protect the business and its shareholders.

The Who's Who: S Corporation Eligibility Demystified

For your business to qualify for S corporation status, it must meet specific criteria. **This includes being incorporated in the United States, in addition to the following:**

- Eligible shareholders include individuals, certain trusts (grantor trusts and electing small business trusts, or ESBTs), and estates.

Partnerships, corporations, and non-resident aliens are, for the most part, ineligible.

- Shareholders must either be citizens or residents of the United States.

- The shareholder count must not exceed 100.

- Issuance of only one class of stock is allowed. All outstanding shares must have the same rights regarding dividends, liquidation, and voting.

- A business can form as a C corporation with a filing status of an S corporation.

- Submitting IRS Form 2553 (Election by a Small Business Corporation) is necessary for the election to be effective, and it must be filed no later than two months and 15 days after the start of the tax year.

- The S corporation election requires unanimous agreement from all shareholders, who must sign and submit the election to the IRS.

- Certain enterprises, like financial institutions and specific investment entities, don't qualify for S corporation election.

- The S corporation must be in good standing with the IRS. If they've previously been disqualified for failure to meet eligibility requirements or because their status was revoked in the past, they may not be eligible now.

The Shareholder's Scale: Weighing Rights and Responsibilities

Shareholders in an S corporation have specific rights and responsibilities defined by the corporation's bylaws, state laws, and federal regulations. Below, **a list of typical rights and responsibilities of shareholders:**

Shareholder Rights

- Ownership in the corporation is proportionate to the number of shares held, which entitles them to the same share of the company's profits and assets.

- Shareholders possess the authority to vote on important company matters, including the election of directors, amendments to bylaws, and critical business decisions.

- They may receive dividends when the company generates profits, as long as the board of directors approves the payment and the company is financially able to do so.

- They can retrieve specific company information, including financial statements, meeting minutes, and other pertinent documents.

- They can transfer their shares to others, unless there are

- restrictions outlined in the company's bylaws or shareholder agreements.

- They may have the opportunity to buy additional shares before the company makes them available to external parties.

Shareholder Responsibilities

- Adherence to the company's bylaws and other governing documents is a requirement.

- Shareholders may be obligated (or highly encouraged) to attend meetings and other important gatherings where decisions affecting the company are made. They can provide input that can influence corporate policies and decisions.

- They're expected to behave ethically and prioritize the corporation's best interests, steering clear of conflicts of interest.

- They consent to pay an agreed-upon price per company share.They may be required to provide consent for certain corporate activities, such as mergers, acquisitions, or changes to the company structure.

- They should maintain accurate records of their stock ownership.

Formality in Function: Upholding Corporate Conventions

A business must comply with certain practices, procedures, and legal requirements expected of all corporations. This is crucial to guarantee transparency, accountability, and adherence to legal requirements. There are a number of corporate conventions they're required to follow. **They must:**

- Regularly review and update the corporate bylaws and other governing documents, ensuring that they accurately reflect the company's structure, rules, and procedures.

- Arrange and conduct mandatory annual meetings for shareholders and directors.

- Keep detailed minutes that include attendees, discussions, decisions, and the results of any votes cast.

- Elect a qualified board of directors who meet regularly to discuss strategic matters, review financial reports, and make key decisions.

- Furnish financial reports promptly and accurately, conducting regular financial audits to verify the integrity of the reporting.

- Keep shareholders informed through regular updates, and offer proxy voting for shareholders who can't attend meetings.

- Establish and uphold a code of conduct for employees, officers, and directors.

- Conduct compliance audits to ensure that the company is adhering to laws and regulations.

- Maintain accurate records of corporate activities.

- Recognize and address potential financial, legal, and other risks connected to the business environment, and obtain appropriate insurance coverages to protect against those risks.

- Ensure that directors, officers, and employees are educated on corporate conventions and industry developments.

S Corps Compared to Other Business Entities

Now let's analyze the commonalities and distinctions between an S corporation and other legal structures.

Partnership vs. S Corporation: A Comparative Analysis

	Partnership	S Corporation
Taxation	Profits and losses are reflected on the individual partner's tax returns. There is no double taxation.	
Liability	General partners have personal liability. Limited Partnerships (LPs) and Limited Liability Partnerships (LLPs) provide protections, but at least one general partner retains personal liability.	Shareholders' personal assets are protected from the debts and liabilities of the business.
Management	Per the partnership agreement, each partner holds a stake in the management of the business.	A board of directors supervises significant decisions and appoints officers accountable for the day-to-day management.

		Shareholders have voting rights for major decisions.
Formation	A partnership agreement outlines the responsibilities and distribution of profits.	The business must file articles of incorporation, adopt bylaws, and elect S corporation status with the IRS.
Ownership	Two or more individuals or entities (known as "partners").	Shareholders who own stock are considered "owners."
Restrictions	Few restrictions on the number and types of partners.	Limit of 100 shareholders, US citizenship and residency requirements, and the types of shareholders are restricted.
Transferability of Interests	Per the terms of the partnership contract.	Transfer of shares must comply with the corporation's bylaws and relevant regulations.

S Corporation and LLC: Distinctive Features

	LLC	S Corporation
Taxation	Can opt to be taxed as a sole proprietorship, partnership, or an S or C corporation.	Profits and losses are reflected on the individual partner's tax returns. There is no double taxation.
Liability	Members' personal assets are protected from business debts and liability.	Shareholders' personal assets are protected from the debts and liabilities of the business.
Management	Members have the option to self-manage or delegate the responsibility of overseeing operations by appointing a manager.	Major decisions are supervised by a board of directors, and officers tasked with day-to-day management are appointed by them. Shareholders have voting rights for major decisions.
Formation	Members agree on the structure. There are no formalities required.	The business must file articles of incorporation, adopt bylaws, and elect S corporation status with the IRS.

Ownership	Members are individuals, other entities, or a combination of both.	Owned by individuals who possess shares of stock in the corporation.
Restrictions	There are few restrictions, making them suitable for a wide range of business and ownership structures.	Limit of 100 shareholders, US citizenship and residency requirements, and restrictions on the types of shareholders.
Transferability of Interests	Varies based on the terms outlined in the partnership agreement.	Transfer of shares must comply with the corporation's bylaws and relevant regulations.
Profit Allocation	Profit and losses are distributed by vote of the members.	Shareholders receive profits according to the proportion of shares they own.

The Corporate Clash: S Corp vs. C Corp

	C Corporation	S Corporation
Taxation	Taxes on profits are paid by the corporation, while individual shareholders are responsible for paying income tax on the dividends they receive. A C corporation has more flexibility with tax planning. They don't have to immediately distribute earnings to shareholders.	Profits and losses are reflected on the individual partner's tax returns. There is no double taxation.
Liability	Shareholders' personal assets are safeguarded from business debts and liabilities.	
Management	A board of directors oversees major decisions and appoints officers responsible for day-to-day management. Shareholders have voting rights for major decisions.	
Formation	C corporations have a formal structure with bylaws, director and shareholder meetings, and adherence to corporate formalities.	The business must be formed as a C corporation by filing articles of incorporation,

		adopting bylaws, and then electing an S corporation status with the IRS.
Ownership	There's a potential for an unrestricted number of shareholders and the issuance of multiple classes of stock.	Owned by individuals who possess shares of stock in the corporation.
Restrictions	There are no limitations on the categories of shareholders.	Limit of 100 shareholders, US citizenship and residency requirements, and the types of shareholders are restricted.
Transferability of Interests	Transfer of shares must comply with the corporation's bylaws and relevant regulations.	
Profit Allocation	The business can distribute profits to shareholders through dividends or retain the earnings within the company.	Shareholders receive profits in accordance with their share ownership.

Myth-Busting: S Corporation Realities

During your research into different business structures, you might've come across information that you remain uncertain about. As is hopefully clear by this point in the book, our purpose is to provide accurate information and clarify any misconceptions.

Dispelling S Corporation Myths

The following are some common myths we've heard regarding S corporations, **contrasted with their reality.**

Myth	Reality
S corporations do not pay taxes.	S corporations are exempt from corporate income tax, but shareholders remain responsible for individual income tax on their respective portions of the company's profits.
S corporations are audited more frequently.	While the IRS will pay attention to an individual's salary versus dividends, S corporations aren't singled out by the IRS for audits.
Only small businesses can be S corporations.	Larger businesses can apply for S corporation status as long as they have 100 or fewer shareholders and meet all other requirements.

S corporations can't have foreign shareholders.	A majority of the shareholders must either be US citizens or residents. Non-resident aliens are generally not eligible, but foreign individuals can be shareholders.
Shareholders can deduct losses exceeding their initial investment.	Shareholders can only deduct losses directly in proportion to their share of the corporation. If the losses exceed this basis, they must be carried forward by the company and used to offset future income.
Shareholders can deduct all business expenses.	Shareholders must follow IRS rules regarding deductions. Personal expenses disguised as business expenses may not be allowed.
S corporations can't have independent contractors.	S corporations can hire independent contractors, but they must also correctly classify workers to avoid tax and legal issues.
S corporations can't accumulate earnings.	While S corporations are generally pass-through entities, they mainly retain some earnings at the corporate level.

S corporations can't own other entities.	S corporations can own subsidiaries and other entities, but their structure must not violate IRS eligibility rules.
S corporation status guarantees tax savings.	Tax savings are not a guarantee, and all businesses are different.
S corporations are always the best choice.	The decision to opt for an S corporation is influenced by various factors, such as the business' nature, ownership structure, and tax considerations.

The S Corporation Spectrum: Benefits and Trade-Offs

With any business formation, there are undeniable advantages as well as aspects that are somewhat less optimal. When selecting a legal entity, it's crucial to assess all aspects.

An S corporation can save you money on taxes, protect your personal assets from business debts and liabilities, provide shareholders who are also employees tax-advantaged benefits, and allow for the deduction of certain business expenses. It can also allow you to raise capital by issuing shares of stock, as well as engage in strategic tax planning by choosing its fiscal year. Plus, changes in ownership will not disrupt the company as a whole.

The S corporation gives up some flexibility with its choice of structure. The 100 shareholder threshold, along with restrictions on who can be a shareholder, may limit investment. The single class of stock restricts flexibility in ownership and distribution, and certain deductions aren't allowed. The IRS can terminate S corporation status if the company fails to maintain eligibility requirements or comply with all regulations. There are strict rules regarding distribution to shareholders, and those shareholders may be subject to the alternative minimum tax (AMT).

When to Pass on an S Corporation

As attractive as S corporation status can seem, there are situations when it might be more prudent to pass on it altogether. If you anticipate having more than 100 shareholders, you have shareholders that don't meet the eligibility requirements, or you wish to issue multiple classes of stock, a C corporation is a better choice. If you wish to retain earnings in the corporation rather than passing the majority of it through to shareholders, the flexibility of a C corporation can offer that option.

If you anticipate losses in the initial years of operation, shareholders might bear the burden. If you're already a C corporation and sell assets within a certain period that might be subject to a gains tax, changing to an S corporation will not negate those taxes.

Finally, if you desire a more simple legal structure with fewer administrative burdens and formalities, an LLC might be more appropriate.

Personal Stake: Unpacking Owner Liability

While shareholders aren't personally liable for a corporation's debts, obligations, or legal liabilities, they still have a personal stake in the organization. Shareholders contribute to the capital of the corporation by purchasing stock, typically intending to see their investment grow. The greater the number of shares an individual possesses, the more significant their stake in the company's success. If the shareholder is also an employee, this stake is even greater. As a result, a shareholder should pay close attention to the inner workings of the company and use their voting power to influence decisions.

Operational Insights: Governance and Roles

Each person involved in an S corporation has a critical role in its success. Let's explore the roles of each member, from the board of directors to the shareholders.

Command and Control: Officers vs. Directors

An S corporation's board of directors oversees the company's management and makes major decisions that control the day-to-day operations. Officers and directors work together to uphold corporate governance, ensure transparency, and remain in compliance with legal and regulatory requirements.

Officers and Their Roles:

- **President/Chief Executive Officer (CEO):** Oversees the overall strategic direction of the company, leads the executive team, makes major decisions, and represents the company in external matters.

- **Vice President(s):** Support the CEO by supervising specific areas, including finance, operations, or marketing.

- **Chief Financial Officer (CFO):** Supervises financial reporting and budgeting, and ensures compliance with financial regulations.

- **Chief Operating Officer (COO):** Responsible for the daily management of operations, including internal processes and procedures.

- **Chief Marketing Officer (CMO):** Oversees marketing strategies, brand development, and promotional activities. They play a key role in driving sales and enhancing market presence.

- **Chief Technology Officer (CTO):** Oversees the company's technological strategy. They may also be responsible for innovation, IT infrastructure, and cybersecurity.

- **Secretary:** Responsible for maintaining corporate records, documenting minutes of meetings, and ensuring compliance with legal requirements.

Note: Corporations are not required to fill all of these roles, and one person can perform multiple duties. S corporations are traditionally required to have a president, vice president, treasurer (CFO), and secretary.

Directors and Their Roles:

- **Chairperson of the Board:** Leads board meetings, facilitates effective communication between the board and management, and may act as the board's representative to the shareholders.

- **Independent Directors:** These individuals are not involved in day-to-day operations, rather serving as an outside perspective to the board. Some of these directors might form committees to audit financial statements, or ensure that executive compensation is aligned with the company's performance and goals.

Share Dynamics: Stock Ownership and Influence

In S corporations, the amount of shares a person owns in the company correlates to their voting power. The greater the number of shares in your possession, the more impact you wield over corporate decisions and how dividends are distributed. Shareholders also elect the board of directors or seek a seat on the board themselves. While the board of directors and officers are seemingly in charge, the real power lies with the shareholders.

Defining Roles: Employees and Shareholders in S Corporations

Understanding the responsibilities of employees and shareholders is essential for effective management and governance of the S corporation. It's important to note that individuals can take on these roles simultaneously.

Employees are responsible for the day-to-day operations, including tasks related to production, service delivery, sales, marketing, finance, human resources, information technology, and more. They must comply with the company's policies and procedures, provide excellent customer service, and interact with other employees and clients.

The ownership stake of shareholders is proportionate to the number of shares they hold in the company. They may vote on matters affecting the corporation, including electing the board of directors and being involved in major corporate decisions. They also monitor the performance of the corporation and engage with the board to stay informed about the company's progress. In return, they receive dividends when the corporation distributes profits.

Inquiries Answered: S Corporation FAQs

As you embark on the journey of establishing an S corporation, you must consider each concept carefully and envision how your company will look in that structure. While this book will give you the necessary basics, your company is unique, and so we recommend taking each concept and determining how it applies to your company. Only at this point will you possess all the necessary information to make a well-informed decision. A great reference to take advantage of is a local office of the Small Business Administration.[2]

State-Specific S Corporation Essentials

While the federal government provides the framework for the taxation and regulation of S corporations, there are also rules and regulations at the state level as well. Before you decide where to file articles of incorporation and open your corporate office, ensure that you research how the state treats S corporations.

For example, different states and municipalities may impose different income tax rates, local taxes, minimum franchise taxes, or other fees. Some may offer credits and incentives to entice you to open your business there. A number of states govern how you handle net operating loss and limitations on how you can carry forward that loss. Additional filing requirements, such as annual reports and statements of information, may apply in other states. Check with your state to see if they follow federal guidelines or if there are local considerations related to ownership. We'll recommend some of the best (and worst) states in which to form an S corp in Chapter Two.

Tax Talk: Deductions and Obligations for Owners

Owners of an S corporation have specific tax deductions and obligations that they need to be aware of. As a pass-through entity, both business income and loss flow to an individual shareholder's personal tax returns. Shareholders are required to report their share of the corporation's income, make estimated tax payments to cover their liability, pay self-employment tax on their wages, report reasonable compensation, and comply with all tax laws.

Owners also want to lower their tax burden as much as possible by taking advantage of allowable deductions. These include health insurance premiums, retirement plan contributions, charitable contributions, interest on business loans, and business expenses such as salaries, rent, utilities, office supplies, and other expenditures directly related to the cost of doing business.

An Exact Step-By-Step Guide to Starting Your S Corp

You'll learn more about ins and outs of S corps as you navigate the rest of this book, but we wanted to give you an all-in-one section you can refer to when it comes to the step-by-step.

Starting an S Corporation is a significant step toward structuring your business for growth, efficiency, and favorable tax treatment. This requires a detailed understanding of the legal and administrative steps to ensure compliance and the optimal setup. S Corporations offer a unique blend of liability protection and tax advantages, including pass-through taxation, which avoids the double taxation often associated with C Corporations.

However, the benefits come with criteria and responsibilities you must adhere to. This section aims to outline a clear guide that will help you through establishing your S Corporation, from the initial brainstorming of your business name to the final touches of compliance and operation.

Choosing a Unique Business Name

Selecting a unique business name is the first step in establishing your S Corporation. It's about creating an identity that resonates with your brand and keeps legal compliance. Begin by searching for name availability within your state's business database, ensuring your chosen name isn't already in use or too similar to existing entities. Additionally, familiarize yourself with state-specific naming rules, which may require certain words to be included or prohibited in your business name. A distinctive, compliant name avoids legal complications and sets the stage for brand recognition and market presence.

Filing Articles of Incorporation

Filing the Articles of Incorporation is next in establishing your S Corporation and legally registering your business within your state. Here's the process:

1. **Gather Required Information:**

- Corporation's name and principal business address.

- Purpose of the business (broadly defined for flexibility).

- Names and addresses of the incorporators.

- Number of shares the corporation is authorized to issue.

2. Prepare the Document:

- Ensure compliance with your state's specific requirements, typically found on the Secretary of State's website.

3. Submit to the Appropriate State Office:

- Most often, this is the Secretary of State's office. Check if online filing is available, but some states may require a physical copy.

4. Understand State-Specific Considerations:

- Filing fees vary by state, from nominal to several hundred dollars.

- Some states may require additional documents or specific information, such as details about the registered agent or operational clauses unique to your business field.

Applying for an Employer Identification Number (EIN)

Obtaining an Employer Identification Number (EIN) is a straightforward step for your S Corporation, acting as its federal tax ID. The IRS makes acquiring an EIN accessible through several methods:

- **Online Application:** The IRS website is the fastest way to get your EIN. This service is available during specific hours and provides an EIN immediately upon completion.

- **Mail or Fax:** You can also apply by sending Form SS-4 to the IRS. Faxing your application speeds up the process slightly, offering a response within a few days, compared to several weeks for mail.

An EIN is needed for various business activities, including opening a bank account, hiring employees, and filing tax returns.

Setting Up a Corporate Bank Account

To set up a corporate bank account for your S Corporation, you'll need several documents:

- Your S Corporation's EIN.

- The Articles of Incorporation.

- A resolution from your board of directors authorizing the opening of the account.

Opening a corporate bank account helps with the financial integrity of your business. It separates personal finances from business transactions, which simplifies accounting and tax preparation. This separation also reinforces the legal distinction between the corporation and its shareholders, essential for maintaining limited liability status.

Electing S Corporation Status with the IRS

Electing S Corporation status gives you access to its tax advantages. This selection involves filing IRS Form 2553. Below are the steps and considerations for this process:

- **Complete IRS Form 2553:** This form requires information about your corporation, including the name, address, EIN, and the tax year's beginning date. All shareholders must consent to the election by signing the form.

- **Filing Deadline:** To be effective for the current tax year, submit Form 2553 no later than two months and 15 days after the beginning of the tax year the election is to take effect, or at any time during the tax year prior.

- Eligibility Criteria:

  o Must be a domestic corporation or entity.

  o Cannot have more than 100 shareholders.

  o Shareholders must be individuals, estates, exempt organizations, or certain trusts.

  o Only one class of stock is permitted.

- Avoid Common Pitfalls:

  o Ensure timely filing; missing the deadline can delay your election until the next tax year.

  o Verify all shareholders sign the form; incomplete submissions can result in rejection.

  o Double-check for compliance with the eligibility criteria to avoid unnecessary complications.

Establishing Bylaws and Shareholder Agreements

Bylaws serve as the internal operating manual for your S Corporation, outlining the structure and governance of your business. They dictate the rules for corporate governance, including the roles and responsibilities of directors and officers, meeting protocols, and shareholder rights. A shareholder agreement complements the bylaws by specifying ownership proportions, dividend distribution policies, and procedures for transferring shares or resolving disputes.

Elements to include in your shareholder agreement are buy-sell provisions, decision-making processes, and conflict resolution mechanisms. Together, these documents provide a framework for your corporation's operation and management.

Organizing the Initial Board of Directors Meeting

The inaugural board of directors meeting is for setting the operational foundation of your S Corporation. Key agenda items include adopting bylaws, electing corporate officers, and approving initial transactions. It's imperative to document decisions and resolutions to maintain comprehensive corporate records. This initial meeting establishes governance practices and demonstrates compliance with corporate formalities, ensuring legal and regulatory adherence.

Complying with State and Local Requirements

Ongoing compliance with state regulations is required for maintaining your S Corporation's good standing. This includes annual report filings, renewing business licenses, and adhering to any specific state mandates regarding corporate operation.

Additionally, understanding local tax obligations and securing necessary business licenses to align with municipal requirements. Proactive management of these responsibilities prevents legal complications and supports continuity.

Key Takeaways

- An S corporation is a legal entity with specific requirements set forth by the IRS.

- An S corporation is composed of a board of directors that directs the company's vision, as well as officers who are in charge of day-to-day operations.

- A major benefit of an S corporation is being able to avoid double taxation.

- An S corporation is complex with specific rules and regulations.

- Choosing a legal structure is only a small aspect of the measure of success in a business.

Chapter 2

Launching Your S Corporation: The Strategic Blueprint

"The way to get started is to quit talking and begin doing."
-Walt Disney, American film producer and entrepreneur

Now that you're equipped with a solid overview of how an S corporation works, it's time to roll up your sleeves and start making some business decisions.

Brand Beginnings: Crafting Your Business Identity

One of the first steps in forming a business (after conceiving of the initial great idea, of course) is to develop your brand. A brand needs to convey your company's values, personality, and core offering to your target audience. A strong business identity helps set your brand apart from the rest of the market and creates a memorable and positive impression. Creating brand guidelines ensures consistency across all communication.

Selecting a Standout Business Name

Before filing paperwork to form an S corporation, it's essential to choose a name for your business. A well-chosen business name creates brand recognition and customer recall, and it contributes to the overall success of your business. Naturally, you must ensure that your chosen name is not only distinctive but also not already registered to any other business entity within the state. There are several factors to consider when selecting a name. **Your business name should:**

- Reflect your brand and values

- Be memorable, emotionally appealing, easy to spell, and easy to pronounce

- Be obtainable as a domain name, enabling you to incorporate it into your website's URL

- Be culturally sensitive and have global appeal

- Be available for trademark registration

- Be available on social media platforms

- Have relevance to your industry and be diverse enough to grow with your business

- Follow your state's naming rules

Registering Your Brand at the State Level

Contact your local secretary of state to register your corporation. They'll need a copy of your articles of incorporation, along with a filing fee. Additionally, you must designate a registered agent. If your business involves the sale of goods, you're required to register for state taxes with the relevant agency. Verify if your state mandates specific licenses and permits for legal operation.[3]

Alternatively, you can use a service such as ZenBusiness, Northwest, Collective, LegalZoom, or Incfile to handle your business set-up. Any one of these can research your name, draft bylaws, secure your employer identification number (EIN), act as your registered agent, and file all required papers with the secretary of state and the IRS. The advantage here is that they provide a comprehensive solution, ensuring that all details are meticulously addressed and finalized. The disadvantage, however, is that these services come with an associated cost. We recommend knowing how all the processes work and then deciding if the expense and time saved is worth it. Ultimately, it's you who's responsible for complying with all rules and regulations.

Securing Your EIN: The IRS Gateway

Every business is required to obtain an Employer Identification Number (EIN from the IRS. An EIN is needed when setting up payroll, opening business bank accounts, building credit, and applying for local permits and licenses. To acquire an EIN, a principal officer, general partner, or owner needs to complete Form SS-4 on the IRS website (www.irs.gov/forms-pubs/about-form-ss-4). The quickest way to apply is online, and there is no associated cost.

Chartering Your Venture: Articles of Incorporation

The articles of incorporation is typically a one-page document with a brief description of your business and purpose, the office address of your corporation, the name and address of a registered agent, and the ownership structure of your corporation, including the number of shares that you'll issue. You can locate the form either online or on the website of your local secretary of state.

Navigating State-Specific Formation Formalities

Formation requirements vary from state to state, and some have specific tax regulations that are different from federal requirements. Many states impose franchise taxes or annual fees on corporations, while others require business licenses or permits depending on the nature of your business. Some states may also have requirements related to corporate formalities, business code compliance, and specific reporting requirements. Contact the secretary of state to ensure that you're compliant with all rules and regulations.

Claiming Your Digital Domain

As suggested above, when it comes to choosing your business name, you should determine whether it's also available as a domain name. After discovering your brand, individuals are likely to attempt to locate your business on the internet. Choosing a website URL, as well as social media handles, that are the same as your corporation name creates consistency and makes you easier to find. Common types of domain names are ".com," ".net," and ".org."

Numerous online resources allow you to check the availability of your chosen name. If the domain isn't available, it may be possible to purchase it from the current owner, but if it is, secure the site using a domain name registrar or a website hosting platform, like Godaddy.com or Bluehost.

At the same time, set up accounts on all social media accounts that you might use in the future—Facebook, Instagram, X (formerly Twitter), LinkedIn, Pinterest, TikTok, Telegram, Snapchat, etc. You want to ensure that your chosen name doesn't get snapped up by someone else on any of these platforms.

Corporate Foundations: Structuring Your S Corp

S corporations require formalities, so take note of the minimum requirements that we'll cover below.

Drafting Your Corporate Bylaws and Agreements

S corporations are required to write and file corporate bylaws, which are a set of rules and regulations that govern the management of your corporation. **Typical items include:**

- How the corporation will appoint and remove board members and officers

- Rules for issuing stock

- Voting

- Schedule of annual meetings

While you can certainly find a form and fill it out, we recommend contacting an attorney to ensure that all areas are covered.

Capital Kickoff: Issuing Initial Stock

After incorporation, it's time to issue stock certificates, whether on paper or electronically. **To qualify or maintain S corporation status, your issuance must meet these requirements:**

- Only one class of stock may be issued (common stock with voting rights)

- Shareholders are required to be citizens or permanent residents of the United States

- Shareholders must be individuals rather than other corporations

To drum up interest in your stock, you may provide a report to potential shareholders with an independent third-party valuation of the stock, but this isn't a hard-and-fast requirement.

Opening the Financial Gates: Your Business Bank Account

Research different banks and financial institutions to find one that'll suit your needs. Be sure to maintain a clear separation between your business and personal finances, as this helps safeguard personal assets and ensures accurate financial reporting.

Some banks cater to small businesses. Factors to consider include fees, account features, FDIC (Federal Deposit Insurance Corporation) or NCUA (National Credit Union Administration) coverage, online banking services, multiple signatories, and branch accessibility. A number of business bank accounts offer ways to facilitate easy tax and financial reporting.

Establish a business checking account for handling day-to-day transactions, bill payments, and receipt of payments. Add a business savings account to set aside money for taxes or dividends, save for business investments, or track surplus funds that'll be used to fund future endeavors.

Gather required materials such as articles of incorporation, business licenses, your EIN, and other legal documents. All signatories on the account should be involved in the account set-up.

Systemizing Success: Record keeping Strategies

Effective record keeping is essential for the smooth operation and compliance of your S corporation. It helps you track financial transactions, ensure compliance with tax regulations, and facilitate corporate governance.

Accounting software is an excellent starting point. This helpful tool can track income, expenses, assets, liabilities, and equity, which will cover the day-to-day financials.

Being an S corporation requires you to retain many documents. These include meeting minutes, corporate resolutions for significant decisions or transactions, employee records, payroll documentation, tax returns and filings, contracts, agreements, corporate bylaws, articles of incorporation, bank and financial statements, insurance policies, intellectual property records, data security and backups, audits and reviews, and so much more. A cloud-based document management solution such as PandaDoc, SharePoint, or OnlyOffice will help you organize these documents and allow you to access them quickly.

Operational Orchestration: Setting the Stage for Success

Now that you have the legalities and structure in place, there are a few more steps to set you up for success, including branding your business identity and defining your purpose, as well as two more legalities: choosing a registered agent and obtaining the proper licenses.

Licensing Your Ambitions

Depending on your business, you may be required to obtain certain licenses to operate. **A few examples:**

- Some state and local governments require a business license just to open their doors.

- Doctors, lawyers, accountants, and architects require a professional license.

- If you're in food service, hospitality, or healthcare, you'll need to comply with health and safety regulations and may require health department permits.

- If you sell tangible goods, you'll need to collect sales tax, which requires a permit.

- Industries involved in manufacturing or hazardous materials may require Occupational Safety and Health Administration (OSHA) permits.

- For physical locations, you may need permits from the fire department to ensure the safety of the building and its occupants.

- Construction and renovation projects require permits from local building departments to ensure compliance with building codes.

Check with state and local government authorities to ensure that you obtain the right permits and licenses.

Designating Your Legal Liaison: Selecting a Registered Agent

A registered agent is either a business or a person who is at least 18 years of age, has a physical address in the state where you do business, and is available (in person) during normal business hours. They'll receive all legal documents, tax forms, government correspondence, and services of process (in the event of a lawsuit) on your business' behalf and forward them to someone in the S corporation in a timely manner.

You can serve as your own agent or select your business as its own registered agent. Keep in mind, however, that registered agents are a matter of public record. If you use your own business, you need to be in complete control of incoming mail to ensure that you don't miss anything. Alternatively, you have the option to enlist the services of a registered agent for a reasonable annual fee.

Branding Your Business Identity

Establishing a strong brand and business identity will distinguish you from your competitors. At this stage, you might've developed your product or service along with your business name. It's at this point that you should start to think about how you want to present your idea to consumers or clients. **Some things to keep in mind:**

- Crafting your brand voice involves determining how you wish to communicate with your customers. Do you want to be viewed as friendly, professional, or innovative?

- Creating taglines, logos, colors, and fonts will further represent your brand. Creating them in the beginning will enable you to display consistency in all marketing materials.

- Identify your target audience and determine the channels and methods through which you'll connect with them. Will you have an online presence, or will you contact them in other forms?

- Be flexible in developing your brand, and have the willingness to change with current market trends.

Mission Crafting: Defining Your Business Purpose

A carefully formulated mission statement articulates the purposes of your business and its objectives. It clarifies your values and defines what distinguishes you from your competitors. If you're one of 100 companies that design widgets, why should a customer buy yours? What sets you apart?

A mission statement should be concise and direct, centering on both the present and the future. It should be specific but flexible enough to grow as your business grows. Simply put, it should align with your business goals. To ensure buy-in, involve key stakeholders—including employees—in the crafting of your mission statement.

Market Mobilization: Preparing for Profit

Now that your business is incorporated, let's look at how you'll structure your operations. Where will you do business—in an office or virtual workspace? How will you attract customers? How do you plan to monitor your expenses and income? But before you address any of those important aspects, you need to sit down and create a business blueprint.

Charting Your Business Blueprint: The Plan

Formulating a thorough plan that delineates your business goals, strategies, **and operational details acts as a roadmap for achieving success.**

1. **Define your business concept.** This includes your mission and vision statements, as well as why customers should choose your business over your competition.

2. **Identify your target audience.** Determine who will buy your product—where they live, what industry they're in, and how you'll reach them.

3. **Develop a catalog of the products and services** your business will offer, including features, benefits, and pricing. Establish how they distinguish themselves from your competitors.

4. **Detail your marketing strategies** for reaching and attracting customers, including digital marketing, content marketing, social media, and traditional advertising. Define how you'll sell your product—a physical storefront, an e-commerce platform, or a combination of both.

5. **Set financial goals and objectives**, including revenue targets, profit margins, and growth projections. Develop a budget that outlines anticipated expenses and revenue streams.

6. **Develop an operations plan** that defines key roles and responsibilities. Plan how you'll recruit, train, and retain employees.

7. **Create a timeline for launch** that outlines all critical events, including marketing campaigns and product releases. Define startup, growth, and expansion phases.

8. **Define how you'll know** that you're successful. Will it be the number of sales, the number of customers, or the first time you turn a profit? Monitor and track metrics to ensure that you're on track with your goals.

9. **Verify that all legal documents** are filed and organized. This includes bylaws, articles of incorporation, and Form 2553 for S corporation tax status.

10. **Consider how you'll communicate** with your internal and external stakeholders.

11. **Consult with key players**—trusted advisors, mentors, and industry experts to ensure that your blueprint grows and adapts to market changes.[4]

Targeting Success: Knowing Your Customers

Getting to know your customers is a fundamental aspect of building and maintaining a successful business. Understanding their needs, preferences, and behaviors allows you to tailor your products and services, improve customer satisfaction, and build lasting relationships. **The following are several ways to get to know your customers:**

- **Ask them questions.** Design surveys and questionnaires asking

- about their pain points, and pay attention to online reviews of your product. Investigate your competitors to understand what aspects make their customers satisfied or dissatisfied.

- **Create a customer persona.** Who makes up your target audience? Where are they located? What's their age range and gender? What values and priorities are significant to them?

- **Use analytics and data** to determine user behavior, including purchase history.

- **Participate in social media.** Pay attention to your customers' feedback and foster meaningful conversations.

- **Attend industry and networking events** to see what's trending and to meet customers in person.

Establishing Your Business Base: Office and Virtual Workspaces

With the widespread availability of fast internet, many companies find success with a remote workforce, but there are advantages to a physical office. An office space allows for in-person collaboration with teams, presents a professional image to customers, and is better able to create a secure environment for sensitive discussions. Some feel that workers are more productive in a focused environment. There are some drawbacks to a physical office space, however, which include overhead expenses such as rent, utilities, maintenance, and furnishings.

Remote or virtual workspaces allow you to cultivate talent from all over the world. Employees like the flexibility of working from anywhere, and it means that you can save on overhead costs. Also, there are countless virtual collaboration tools and technologies that encourage teamwork and camaraderie.

A combination of physical and virtual workspace allows for partial work-from-home opportunities for employees as well as a space to gather for collaboration. Whichever one you choose, keep the needs of the client in mind and ensure that you're meeting all regulatory requirements regarding labor laws and data security.

Financial Foresight: Accounting Systems

Choosing an easy-to-use accounting system that'll perform all the functions needed is crucial. **Numerous effective systems are available, and you'll want to select one that:**

- Generates customer invoices

- Logs accounts receivable upon invoicing a customer

- Creates payroll records

- Matches records to transactions during bank reconciliations

- Backs up and secures your records, either on a hard drive or in the cloud

Examples of accounting systems that are easy to get up and running are QuickBooks, FreshBooks, and Wave Accounting.

Crafting Your Online Ecosystem

Given that a significant number of individuals rely on the internet for information, your business will benefit greatly from an online presence. After purchasing a domain, as mentioned earlier, the next step is to design your website.

Constructing Your Digital Storefront: The Website

A website can serve many purposes, including telling your customers about your corporation, who your board members and directors are, and outlining your products and services. It should be user-friendly with clear and compelling call-to-actions (CTAs). You can add content to your website to educate your customers, and it should also integrate with your social media platforms.

We recommend that you work with a designer who can incorporate your branding fundamentals, create elements that appeal to your target audience, optimize the website to show up high in search engine ranks, and tie in analytics so that you can determine how successful your website is in attracting clicks.

Selecting a Strategic State for Incorporation

Most businesses file articles of incorporation where they have their primary office, but others may choose a state that's more business-friendly in terms of lower tax rates, favorable corporate laws, and fewer regulatory burdens.

For example, many large corporations are formed in Delaware because it has well-established corporate laws and a specialized court for business-related disputes. There's no state sales tax and no corporate income tax for Delaware corporations not operating in the state (a big advantage for C corporations). Since so many corporations reside in Delaware, investors are more familiar with the state's laws and enjoy doing business in familiar territory. That said, the drawbacks include added expenses, and most of the benefits gained are for large corporations with many shareholders.

Another popular state for incorporation is Nevada. There are no state taxes, and Nevada values privacy—it doesn't require you to list the names of directors on your articles of incorporation. You're also not required to list company corporate assets for the state, which further protects you from liability. The drawbacks to incorporating in Nevada, however, include high fees and a stigma attached to the state's reputation because of its...

Corporations also consider Wyoming due to its low taxes, flexibility in business structure, and lower expenses, but drawbacks include fewer benefits for remote businesses.

Several states that consistently make the Top 10 Lists for incorporation are South Dakota, Florida, Montana, New Hampshire, and Alaska. In addition, other states that offer tax benefits include Colorado, Arkansas, Iowa, Kentucky, Michigan, Mississippi, Missouri, New Mexico, and Tennessee.

Some less-desirable states in which to form corporations include New Jersey, New York, California, Connecticut, and Maryland, as their drawbacks include higher tax rates, unfavorable cost of commercial property, and simply more hoops to jump through.

Carefully consider your business needs and goals to see if the state in which you reside is a good choice for your industry.

Regulatory Rigor: Compliance Mastery

Navigating and mastering the regulatory requirements requires diligence and proper planning. At this point, you should have a list of rules and regulations that you must follow at the federal, state, and local levels. If you have any questions about what each requirement entails, ask questions now. Be aware that new laws, amendments, or updates to regulations change periodically, so monitor these changes and adjust your timelines to stay in compliance.

To ensure that you have the proper documentation, set up a secure recordkeeping and document-storage system. Develop policies, procedures, and controls, and make sure that all your employees adhere to them. Set up internal audits and monitor compliance at all levels, and always seek legal advice when navigating complex regulatory issues.

Situating Your S Corp: Location Logistics

Ensure that you choose to locate your S corporation near the materials you need to produce your product, or near your customers. For example, if you require large amounts of raw material to produce your product, you can either locate your office or plant near the source of the raw material or somewhere where it's easy to deliver the product. And if your customers frequent your location, make sure that it's easily accessible.

Supply Chain and Staffing

Depending on the type of business you operate, you're likely to need materials for development and manufacturing, as well as people to produce the product or service. Let's dive into the intricacies of this combination.

Networking with Suppliers and Vendors

Building strong and sustainable business relationships with suppliers and vendors can foster the growth and success of your business. When working with a supplier, establish clear lines of communication and define expectations. Sign contracts for price and supply, and seek out suppliers and vendors with a proven track record of reliability. Know where their product comes from and check for consistent quality. Ensure that your supplier or vendor aligns with your ethical standards, and make sure that they'll be able to keep up with your increasing demand.

In the event that there's a break in the supply chain, establish strategies that'll mitigate the impact on your business, including identifying alternative suppliers. One supplier can offer volume discounts, but multiple suppliers can diversify risk.

Connecting Your Communication Lifelines

The success of your business hinges on the effectiveness of your internal and external communication. Internally, all employees need a unified platform with which to communicate. This involves utilizing identical email, instant messaging, video conferencing, and project management tools. Set up an intranet in which internal communications are accessed, and encourage open communication between teams so that everyone is on the same page. In the event of an emergency, develop a communications plan to check in and notify all employees and stakeholders of events and actions. Some of the more popular tools to encourage sharing and communication between team members are Asana and Slack.

Talent Acquisition and Team Building

Building a successful workforce is vital. To attract and retain talent that sufficiently aligns with your business goals, you need to first define each job role and create a compelling job description. Offer a competitive compensation and benefits package, and use a variety of recruitment channels to reach a diverse pool of candidates. Build a talent pipeline and encourage current employees to refer applicants as well. Create a streamlined and effective screening process to select the best candidates.

Once individuals are onboard, build a cohesive team by:

- Establishing clear roles and responsibilities

- Defining clear team goals

- Cultivating a positive work environment

- Encouraging collaboration

- Providing professional development opportunities

- Implementing feedback

- Creating a recognition program

- Using each person's strengths where they're best needed

How to Price Your Products and Services

One of the more challenging aspects of running a business is pricing your products and services. Price a product too low and you aren't going to earn enough to cover your costs, and yet you might alienate customers if you set the price too high.

The initial step is to ascertain the cost of producing your product or delivering your service. Take into consideration direct costs (material and labor) as well as indirect costs (overhead and marketing). Calculate your break-even point to understand the minimum revenue needed to cover costs, then compare these costs against your competition. If they're significantly lower, you can either cut costs or differentiate your product based on quality, innovation, or convenience to the customer.

Additional factors to contemplate when establishing pricing include incorporating promotions and discounts to stimulate interest. Subscription or membership models foster customer loyalty, and they're a great way to create recurring revenue.

Financing Your S Corporation Vision

Whether your business can sustain itself depends on money. Unless you have guaranteed revenue right out of the gate, you're going to have to look into financing. Securing the necessary funding is crucial to cover operational expenses, expand into new markets or product lines, and capitalize on business opportunities.

S corporations are comprised of shareholders—the original investors in your company. Other funding sources include angel investors, venture capitalists, private equity firms, bank loans, lines of credit, crowdfunding, government grants and subsidies, and bootstrapping (using personal savings or profits from the company to fund initial operations and growth). Regardless of the method selected, ensure that all financial activities adhere to legal and regulatory requirements. Seek professional advice if there are any questions as to whether the S corporation's status will be affected by the funding source.

Key Takeaways

- It's critical to choose a strong business name and develop your brand identity.

- There are specific steps to ensure that your S corporation is set up for success, including filing articles of incorporation, choosing a registered agent, filing the right forms with the IRS, and following a well-thought-out business roadmap.

- Your success is dependent upon choosing the right operating location, suppliers, vendors, and employees.

- Customers are your most valuable resource, so you should spend time understanding their needs, how you can reach them through marketing channels, and how you can differentiate yourself from the competition.

- There are several options for financing your corporate ventures, as long as they follow the S corporation rules and regulations

Chapter 3

Building Your S Corporation from the Ground Up

"You don't build a business. You build people, then people build the business."

-Zig Ziglar, American author and entrepreneur

At this point, we've covered forming an S corporation and the requirements to comply with state and federal regulations. We've also touched a little on how to structure your office, as well as options for your choice of software. Now we'll dig deeper into some more intricate details—such as what goes into choosing your management team, developing a branding strategy, and setting up your operations.

Building Your S Corp Board and Team

For an S corporation to operate, it must have a board of directors and officers. The number of these depends on how large or small your business is and what your state requires.

Handpicking Your Leadership: Officers and Directors

Board members are handpicked by the person who forms the corporation. This person may also be the president or CEO, and in some cases, the CEO is also the chairman of the board. In fact, in some states, one person can fulfill all the director and officer roles, but other states might require a minimum of one director and one officer.

While a single individual can handle multiple roles, it's important to consider the challenges associated with this, such as the need for checks and balances in decision making and the potential for conflicts of interest. If you choose directors and officers other than yourself, select directors who can provide guidance and make decisions for the company, and choose officers that'll help you run the day-to-day operations.

Directors are typically not paid (except for expenses required to complete their role), although the bylaws can stipulate a fee for their service. Incentives to be a director include their vested interests as a shareholder, as well as networking opportunities and the ability to shape the strategic direction of a company.

Officers are employees of the company and should be compensated fairly. Your bylaws should clearly outline the number of directors and their duties.

Share Dynamics: Allocating the Lifeblood of Your S Corp

In an S corporation, shareholders are required to be either US citizens or resident aliens, and the number of shareholders is restricted to a maximum of 100. These could be founders, key employees, family members, or investors. Select shareholders whose values and strategic alignment resonate with the company's direction and vision. Look for individuals who bring value in terms of finances, but also expertise, industry connections, or relevant skills.

Shareholders will be involved in making key decisions with the board, so you want individuals who are committed to the success of the business. Also, keep in mind that the number of shares that an individual holds directly correlates to their voting influence.

Blueprints of Success: Crafting Your Corporate DNA

In simple terms, bylaws and accounting principles lay the foundation for your corporate structure.

Penning Bylaws and Agreements

Bylaws describe the standard operating procedures for your company, laying out important information regarding board and shareholder meetings, voting rights, responsibilities, quorums, and more. They're one of the first documents written and approved by the board of directors.

While bylaws are only required by 31 states, it's a very helpful document to ensure that the company is following S corporation laws and that everyone is on the same page.

How to Create Bylaws:

- Gather individuals tasked with the incorporation of the business. Select the leaders of the organization (usually a two-third majority is required).

- Select board members. Often, members with the most shares of the company are nominated to be on the board.

- Create the rules of the organization, including how business decisions will be made, when and where annual meetings will occur, the percentage of shareholders required to decide (also known as a quorum), when and how dividends will be paid, and the roles assigned to each member.

- Write the actual bylaws. There are templates available online, and companies exist that will assist you with the legal jargon.

- In most states, a secretary or other administrative official must sign the bylaws for them to go into full effect.

With those crucial steps completed, you're now ready to begin business operations.

Record Keeping For You S Corp

An S corporation has the option to employ various accounting methods, including cash, accrual, or a blend of both. The difference is when an income or expense is accounted for. Cash-basis accounting records income at the time of receipt, and it records expenses when they're paid. The accrual method enters the income when it's invoiced, and it enters the expenses when you're billed for them.

Your accounting system should track:

- Assets (such as cash on hand, inventory, property, plant equipment, patents, and copyrights)

- Liabilities (including short- and long-term debt, accounts payable, deferred taxes, and accrued expenses)

- Owner's equity (the owner's and shareholder's interest in the business, including their initial investment, retained earnings, and other capital invested)

- Revenue from sales, service, or interest from investment or bank accounts

- Costs associated with revenue generation (such as rent, utilities, salaries, and marketing expenses)

- Cost of goods sold (this represents the expenses linked to the production of goods or services)

- Profits and losses resulting from the sale of assets

- Tax expenses (such as franchise taxes required by some states)

A solid reference for ensuring that you're following proper accounting principles is the AICPA (Association of International Certified Personal Accountants).[5]

License to Operate: Securing Your Business Legitimacy

An S corporation doesn't require a license to do business, but most states do require a general business license. The state might require licenses or permits based on your type of business (such as professional licenses for law or medical companies) and permits for transportation, health, environmental, and sales-based licenses or permits.

Obtain all licenses and permits prior to opening your business and initiating customer transactions.

The Agent Advantage: Your Regulatory Representative

It's common for someone in an S corporation to specialize in regulatory matters. Commonly called a compliance officer, regulatory affairs specialist, or other similar title, this person monitors changes in regulations, implements policies and procedures to ensure compliance, and serves as a point of contact for regulatory authorities.

Whether you have an official person in charge of monitoring regulatory compliance or you handle this role yourself, it's important to ensure that you're following all rules and regulations set forth by state and federal agencies.

Branding and Vision: The Pillars of Public Image

The way you present your product or service to the public significantly influences your success as a business. Branding and vision aren't just buzzwords—they're stepping stones necessary to build trust and loyalty.

Crafting Your Corporate Identity: Logo and Branding

A strong corporate identity means carefully choosing how your company looks and communicates. A big part of this is designing a unique logo that reflects your company's mission and is easy to remember. Your logo serves as the face of your company, and it should mirror your identity and character. In addition, the colors and feel of your logo should carry forward to your website, social media, business cards, and any other customer-facing collateral. A unified and professional look creates a positive and lasting impression.

Visioneering: Your Mission Statement and Business Compass

Your company's vision defines the overarching purpose and direction of your business. Think of your vision as how you want your company to look in the future by considering the long-term goals and how you plan to get there. Bring in your stakeholders, including employees and leadership, to brainstorm the company's future aspirations.

After you define your vision statement, it's crucial that you use it in your strategic planning process. Don't be afraid to modify or revise it as changes in the industry unfold. Your vision statement serves as a guiding compass, leading you and your business in a unified direction.

Market Mastery: Zeroing in on Your Audience

Identifying and connecting with your target audience involves a great deal of study, both into human behavior and the atmosphere of the market in which you've chosen to sell. This might involve defining your buyer's persona—your ideal customer in terms of demographics, interests, challenges, and buying behavior. If you've already started selling (or at least generating interest in) your offerings through social channels, collect information regarding your buyer's preferences and what attracted them to your brand. You may have an opportunity to engage with them directly to determine what they need or want, and this unique situation may give you a leg up on your competitors. The goal is to craft a set of buyer personas with which you understand their demographics (age, gender, and location), their professional status (job title, industry, and income level), their values and beliefs, their pain points (frustrations, obstacles, and drivers of action), and where they like to spend their time online. This allows you to create products for—and market to—these types of people specifically. If it helps, you can even give a name to each persona to really personalize them.

Establishing Your Business Operations

Fostering collaboration among your shareholders, officers, and employees depends on a multitude of factors, including where they work.

Setting the Stage: Office Spaces and Virtual Places

Setting up an office, whether at a physical location or in a virtual environment, involves thoughtful planning and execution. In the previous chapter, we explored the pros and cons of each setting, all of which hinge on your type of business. If you have customers who come into the office for face-to-face meetings, your office environment will look much different than one employing a workforce that largely works independently.

Can you provide the same level of service to employees who work all over the world, or do you desire in-person collaboration? There are endless possibilities when setting up a physical location—offices with doors for privacy, cubicles that encourage a more social environment, or an open-office system where there are no assigned spaces.

If you decide to offer your employees remote opportunities, how will that look? There are a myriad of collaboration tools, communication platforms, and project management systems that promote unity while giving employees a level of freedom, such as Asana, Trello, and Slack.

The Accountant's Canvas: Painting Your Financial Picture

You're less likely to achieve the success you desire without having a strong, systematic approach to finances. S corporations report to shareholders, and they're in the business of making money. Without the ability to pay officers and employees, purchase needed supplies, reach customers, and provide the infrastructure allowing you to support these processes, shareholders will have serious reservations about your leadership ability.

A solid business plan with specific financial goals—and steps on how your company will achieve those goals—will set minds at ease. Provide clear financial statements with projected income and expenses, as well as inside and outside financing.

Crafting a Compelling Online Persona

The web is your indispensable link to your customers, and so reaching the customers that would benefit most from your offering is crucial. After all, how good is your product or service if no one buys it—or even knows about it?

A thoughtfully developed online persona will resonate with your intended audience, pulling at their heartstrings and creating a sense of urgency. It'll fill a need. You can do this by defining the purpose and image you want to convey, and then creating visuals that reflect your personality. Share content that they want to learn about. Share your experiences. Get personal. However, don't forget to ensure that you're sticking with your brand values.

For example, if your business sells higher ticket products ($3k and above), you'll want to ensure that your persona has a premium feel in terms of the way you communicate, the language you use, how your website is built and functions, and how you create content (if you promote on platforms like Instagram, YouTube, etc.). In that case, here's a great question to ask before recording a piece of content: "Would someone seeing this want to pay me $10k? If not, how can I clean it up in a way where that would be the case?"

Compliance and Location for Your S Corp

Staying in compliance can be tricky. Ensure that you're researching tax laws, economic activities, and legal regulations before choosing a location in which to set up your business, and stay abreast of any future changes that may occur.

Staying Ahead of Compliance

Evolving laws, rules, and regulations can pose a challenge, so appoint an individual within your organization to monitor these changes. They can do this by subscribing to industry publications, participating in professional networks, and attending relevant workshops or seminars. You should also maintain contact with legal professionals or consultants specializing in business regulations.

When a change comes along that affects your industry, plot a course of action to guarantee compliance. Ensure that all parties understand the significance of the proposed changes. Make use of internal audits, as they can assess levels of compliance and identify areas for improvement.

Location Scouting

When a business has a physical presence in a particular location—whether it's your office, a storefront, a warehouse, or the location of your employees—that business is tied to its particular jurisdiction and is, therefore, obligated to pay taxes. Therefore, before setting up any operations, determine that you're aware of the tax laws and economic activities of that area.

It's important to understand that it's not only the physical location that determines the business nexus—it also comes down to a threshold of sales, revenue, or transactions that occur in that jurisdiction. This comes into consideration when a business is involved in e-commerce or remote sales, and so in that case, investigate all possible obligations.

Supply Chain and Communications: Building Your Business Backbone

Let this be your mantra of sorts: Coordination and collaboration across an organization requires good communication. Establish clear channels between employees, shareholders, suppliers, and vendors. This backbone will ensure a solid foundation and enable your business to be agile and effective when navigating complexities.

Partnering with Suppliers and Vendors

Suppliers and vendors play crucial roles in the supply chain and operational efficiency, and fostering strong partnerships can lead to shared growth and prosperity. You might choose a supplier or vendor because of their raw materials, price, or terms, but the relationship can be so much more advantageous to both parties. The success of your business trickles down into growth for your suppliers.

Once a trusted relationship is established, it can grow as you expand your offerings. Instead of looking for a new supplier, partner with your current one and see what they can do in terms of innovation, streamlining processes, or strategic alignment. Perhaps your supplier has some innovative ideas that can benefit your business as well. By working together, businesses can help build resilient and sustainable supply chains.

Establishing Information Pathways

Internal and external communications are vital in maintaining smooth operations. Establishing information pathways involves not only technology platforms but also the methods of communication between individuals. For example, when working on a project, do you expect a chain of command to be followed, or is there an open-door policy to the top? If an employee has an idea that's outside of the norm, should they schedule a chat or formulate a document?

Determining the "who" and "how" regarding communication with customers, vendors, and suppliers sets expectations for both sides. Smooth information flow across all levels of the organization enhances its overall success and adaptability in the business environment.

Fostering a Foundation of Talent

A plan is only as good as its execution, and to achieve this effectively, you need a skilled workforce. Choose individuals that align with your goals and are team players.

Talent Scouting: Crafting Your Crew

Talent scouting is the process of identifying, recruiting, and cultivating skilled individuals to form a cohesive and high-performing team. It goes without saying, but talent is crucial for the success of any organization. You could advertise on job boards and screen candidates in-house, or you could hire a talent agency to recruit and screen candidates for you. This approach will cost a bit more, but it might offer you a more diverse group of candidates. You could also ask your friends, colleagues, employees, or shareholders for referrals.

Whichever way you choose, be deliberate in your process. Create job descriptions outlining clear roles and responsibilities. Understand your expectations for the job, including salary and behaviors. Picture your ideal candidate, but remain flexible. Also, it's key to ensure that your benefits package is in line with the industry.

Below are a few hidden red flags to look for in the hiring process (if a candidate has these, be wary!):

- Slow response times (taking more than a day to respond to emails and other correspondence)

- Lack of reliability (needing to reschedule, even once, or showing up late even by a minute, etc.)

- Failing the "vibe check" (something about their energy or presence just doesn't sit well with you, or maybe you feel like they won't mesh well with your company culture—trust your instincts!)

Mastering Your Monetary Strategy

To position your offerings in the market, it's important to understand the value that they bring to your customers. To achieve this, you need to conduct some research into what your competitors are offering and how they're perceived by the market. Study production costs, market demand, and different price points. Find your sweet spot. Next, contemplate seasonal promotions, discounting tactics, and bundling (providing multiple products for a single price). Don't be afraid to experiment, but understand how your price affects your bottom line.

Financial Framework: Capitalizing on Your Vision

A financial framework is the strategic foundation that helps you achieve your goals. It involves structuring financial strategies, budgeting, and resource allocation to align with the organization's goals, enabling the realization of its vision through prudent financial management and strategic investments.

Monetary Mechanisms: Securing Your Fiscal Foundation

Establishing a solid monetary foundation begins with budgeting, including planning and monitoring each inflow and expenditure. This involves a clear understanding of operational costs, capital expenditures, and revenue projections. Also, you'll definitely want to have a strong grasp of cash flow.

Investment strategies, debt management, and financial forecasting enhance your business' fiscal stability. Risk management ensures that you're prepared for market fluctuations and economic uncertainties.

A solid foundation, as well as reporting and auditing processes, will ensure that you can weather any storm that comes your way, and it sets you up for long-term success.

The Promotional Blueprint

Solid marketing strategies ensure that you're reaching customers and making sales. Among these strategies is the promotional blueprint, which encompasses digital platforms, traditional advertising, public relations, and social media. The promotional blueprint is a dynamic and adaptable guide to ensure that marketing strategies are aligned with business goals.

Each of these marketing channels is used to maximize visibility and engagement, with a strong focus on reaching your customers during milestone events and product launches. Along with planning for the event, following through afterwards measures the success of the campaign. For example, let's say that you run a Black Friday sale for your product. You could do an Instagram Story, Reel, and Post, along with an email launch sequence to promote it over the course of those few days. Then, you could measure metrics like the clicks, sales, and conversion rate. Just make sure not to run huge sales too often, as these can dilute your brand and train your customers to only sign up when they get a discount!

Tax Tactics: Steering Through State and Local Levies

Earlier, we considered the tax implications of your chosen jurisdiction. As you start to make sales, you'll want to employ tax strategies to ensure that you comply but not overpay. The initial step involves understanding the various types of taxes and the governing body responsible for their collections. It's essential that you explore tax credits and incentives offered by your state or locality.

Meticulous record keeping helps with compliance and provides a basis for strategic tax planning. Streamline tax automation using technology like QuickBooks. Engaging with tax authorities, responding promptly to inquiries, and asking questions on ambiguous tax issues will ensure that there are no surprises on the tax front.

Growth and Governance: Charting the Future

As a company expands, its structures, policies, and practices play a pivotal role in steering the course of its development. Governance ensures responsible growth management, alignment with organizational goals, and adherence to regulatory requirements. A well-balanced approach to growth and governance positions it for long-term success by creating a resilient and adaptable framework for the future.

Fueling Your Initial Growth Spurt

Unless you have a big nest egg, you'll need a plan for obtaining financial support and strategic resources. Securing seed funding from investors, forming strategic partnerships, and embracing frugality are the foundational elements that fuel the early stages of expansion. You may also explore avenues such as venture capitalism, crowdfunding, and government grants. And, obviously, don't forget about your shareholders—the initial investors in your business. Just be careful who you hand out equity to and how, especially early on. If you're going to offer equity, it should be for a great reason, and one that you anticipate benefiting the business long-term.

Mapping Out Business Expansion

As your business grows, you'll need to continually stay ahead of trends and focus on providing value for your customers. After capturing the customer's interest, concentrate on upselling to encourage repeat business. Find out what they need, and use the power of innovation, strategic partnerships, and brand marketing to map out an expansion plan that aligns with your goals. For example, let's say that you have a supplement company, and your customer buys your creatine supplement. After they enter their info on the purchase page, they could be redirected to another page where you sell whey protein—or where you sell another company's whey protein and get a cut of the sale as an affiliate. These are two related products—if they take creatine, they likely work out consistently, and if that's the case, they likely have a need for whey protein. Capitalize on anticipating your customer's needs by aligning your offerings accordingly. You can also upsell other related products in your follow-up email sequence. Athletic Greens is a great example of this. The company has its main product (the healthy greens powder you've likely heard about), along with a host of other items such as fish oil, vitamin D, and whey protein. Most customers come for the greens powder, but then are gradually introduced to Athletic Greens' other products. This is part of the reason they've gone from a small company to one worth over a billion dollars!

Legal Landmarks: Navigating the Corporate Legal Landscape

Legal landmarks are important points in a company's journey. These include starting the business, following rules, and making contracts for important things like mergers and protecting ideas. As the business grows, it must follow industry rules, as well as employment and contract laws. By navigating these legal landmarks carefully, a business can reduce risks, foster transparency, and establish a solid legal foundation that supports long-term growth.

Key Takeaways

- Choose the right shareholders, board members, and officers that align with your corporation's mission.

- Create a solid backbone by drafting bylaws and setting up accounting systems.

- Craft your market presence with a catchy logo, a well-thought-out branding strategy, and targeted social media posts.

- Develop strategic relationships with suppliers and vendors.

- Be aware of the tax implications of your location.

- Build a solid workforce with effective talent scouting.

- Raise capital and prepare for future growth.

Chapter 4

Simple Tax Tips for S Corporations

"While some people might find it distasteful to pay taxes, I don't. I
find it patriotic."
-Mark Cuban

The Pass-Through Tax Phenomenon

A major benefit of S corporations is pass-through taxation. C
corporations are taxed on income at both the corporate and individual
levels, but S corporations pass all the income through to their
shareholders, thus avoiding the tax at the corporate level. This
framework is the main attraction of an S corporation—it encourages
investment and growth. Decoding Pass-Through Taxation: A Windfall
for S Corp Owners

As an owner of an S corporation, you can pass through income to your
personal tax return. Depending on the amount of profit and loss, this
could be very advantageous, especially if the individual tax rates are less
than the corporate ones.

The S corporation, in turn, saves on corporate tax liabilities, meaning
that the owners benefit from the corporation's financial success. In
addition, owners can claim tax credits generated by the corporation. The
S corporation can also distribute profits and losses according to
shareholder percentages, which allows for the optimization of individual
tax situations.

Payroll vs. Dividends: Crafting Your Compensation Strategy

Payroll is the regular salaries or wages that are subject to employment taxes. Dividends, on the other hand, are shareholder distribution. An employee can also be a shareholder, in which case they'll receive both wages and dividends.

Employees must be paid a fair wage, and the rest of the compensation can be paid in dividends. But be careful of the percentage—the IRS uses the term "reasonable compensation," which is highly subjective. Some factors to consider include the nature of the duties performed, the intricacies of the job, the cost of living in the area where your business operates, compensation relative to the business' gross and net income, and the individual's salary history.

Tactics to Avoid Double Taxation

By its very nature, an S corporation avoids double taxation, but only as long as it meets IRS guidelines.

C corporations are taxed at the corporate level. They pay taxes on their profits and losses, and then may or may not pay a dividend to their shareholders, who are then taxed on those dividends. Essentially, the profits are taxed twice. In exchange, C corporations enjoy a high level of freedom and flexibility when it comes to running their business.

An S corporation, however, sidesteps double taxation. Taxes are still paid to the proper authorities, but in a different way. At the end of the fiscal year, the S corporation passes profits and losses to the shareholders. Profits are taxed once, at the shareholder level. Depending on the circumstances, this may lead to noteworthy tax savings.

Deductions and Credits for S Corporations

Exploring the deductions and credits available to S corporations is worthwhile, as it has the potential to significantly reduce your tax obligations and save you a considerable amount of money.

Lowering taxable income is the goal of an S corporation and its shareholders, **and they can do this by taking advantage of all deductions they qualify for, including:**

- Business expenses (such as rent, utilities, salaries, and office supplies)

- Salaries and wages paid to employees

- Employee perks (such as health insurance, retirement plans, and various other fringe benefits)

- Start-up costs incurred in the initial phases of business operations

- Interest paid on loans or debts

- Charitable contributions

- Home office deductions (if the company runs out of the owner's home)

- Travel expenses (including hotels, meals, and car rentals)

- Depreciation of equipment and vehicles

The Art of Tax Benefit Maximization

Maximizing tax benefits involves understanding how the S corporation works, how profits are allocated, and how to sync tax timelines.

Crafting Your S Corporation Tax Strategy: A Tactical Approach

Taxes can be complicated, but there are a few things that S corporations can do to optimize their strategy. Section 199A deduction permits S corporations to deduct up to 20% of their qualified business income. Research and Development credits offer an opportunity for additional cash flow, and charitable donations can effectively lower tax burdens.[6]

On the personal side of things, we've already mentioned paying yourself a reasonable salary, as doing this minimizes self-employment taxes and ensures IRS compliance. Hiring family members, writing off home expenses (if your home is your office), deducting health insurance premiums, maximizing retirement contributions, and taking advantage of all available deductions for expenses can all reduce your tax burden.

Syncing Your S Corp with Tax Timelines

Paying taxes on time avoids penalties, and so it's recommended that you keep a tax calendar to ensure that you don't miss any deadlines. Most tax filings require prior planning with meticulously organized financial records. More importantly, tax obligations should be well-thought-out so that they minimize stress, maximize deductions, and position your S corporation for financial success. Keep up with tax laws and business dynamics to ensure that your tax timelines remain in sync with your goals.

On the shareholder side, shareholders will file individual tax returns, which are due April 15th of each year. Shareholders may be required to file quarterly tax returns depending on their liabilities. Although it isn't a direct obligation, the S corporation furnishes shareholders with Schedule K-1, outlining each shareholder's portion of the corporation's income, deductions, credits, and other relevant items.

If you need extra time to file your taxes, the IRS can issue an extension until October 15th of the same year, but in order to avoid penalties and interest on taxes owed, you need to pay any taxes owed by the original filing deadline.

Asset Economics: Depreciation and Amortization

If your company has assets, utilizing strategies such as depreciation and amortization can save you money on your taxes.

The Depreciation Deduction Dimension: Slashing Taxes on Assets

Physical assets such as machinery, buildings, vehicles, and equipment have a limited lifespan for your business. S corporations can reduce taxes on these assets by carefully tracking their gradual wear and tear. Important factors include correctly categorizing assets, strategically timing purchases to get maximum deductions, and exploring options like bonus depreciation and Section 179 expensing for instant tax advantages.

Depreciation strategies can also include discerning between routine maintenance and capital improvements. Savings due to depreciation can then be strategically reinvested into business growth and development.

Common methods include straight-line depreciation, declining balance, or units of production. The formula for straight-line depreciation, for example, is (Cost - Salvage Value)/Useful Life.

Amortization Tactics: Stretching Expenses Over Years

Amortization involves spreading the cost of an intangible asset—such as a patent, trademark, or goodwill—over a specific period. This process serves to match the expenses of acquiring the asset with the revenue it generates over its lifespan.

Similar to leasing a car or a building space, a business can lease the use of a brand or a trademark instead of going through the process to create their own.

Other options that work along the same lines are loan financing, subscription services, or deferred payments. Breaking down projects into stages and spreading the cost over several fiscal periods can offer financial flexibility and help with cash flow management.

Let's say that you purchase a patent for a new technology for $100,000, and the patent is estimated to have a useful life of 10 years. You would amortize the cost of the patent by spreading the $100,000 over its useful life, which means that $10,000 would be expensed each year.

This annual expense of $10,000 would be recorded on the income statement as an amortization expense, reducing the company's net income. Meanwhile, the value of the patent on the balance sheet would decrease by $10,000 each year until the patent's useful life is exhausted, at which point its value would be reduced to zero.

Charitable Ventures and Tax Rewards

Philanthropy helps other organizations, but it can also maximize your tax benefits. In other words, you can harness your charitable contributions to assist with your overall bottom line—as well as improve your business' public persona.

Balancing Benevolence and Benefits in Charitable Giving

Donating to charity is a wonderful way to support causes and create a positive image for your company. Pick organizations that align with your company's mission, and make sure that your contributions match your values. Partnering with reputable groups boosts the impact of your giving, and involving employees and stakeholders creates a sense of shared purpose. Always make ethical choices, avoiding situations in which benefits could harm recipients. Being active in the community and adapting to changing needs shows a commitment to understanding and respecting different cultures.

Making Contributions Count: Charitable Strategy for S Corps

While S corporations themselves don't receive direct tax deductions for charitable donations, shareholders can individually benefit by deducting their share of the corporation's contributions on their personal tax returns. This pass-through deduction provides a financial incentive for philanthropy.

Allowable deductions include contributions to religious organizations, non-profit schools and hospitals, governments, veteran's groups, and other organizations that can accept tax-deductible contributions. The deduction is limited to 20-50% of the corporation's adjusted gross income, depending on the donation recipient. The donation is treated as a deduction on the shareholder's tax return.

For example, if an S corporation has two equal shareholders and they

donate $5,000 to a charitable organization, each shareholder will be able to deduct $2,500 on their personal tax returns. How much each shareholder saves depends on their tax bracket, but if they were taxed at 20%, they'd save $500 from this deduction alone.

Beyond tax advantages, charitable giving allows S corporations to actively contribute to community well-being, enhancing corporate reputation and fostering positive relationships with customers, employees, and the local community. Additionally, involvement in charitable activities can yield networking opportunities, sponsorship benefits, and positive brand associations.

Bulletproof Tax Record Keeping

Keeping thorough tax records is vital for individuals and businesses to meet compliance requirements. The last thing you want is to come up short during tax season by not being diligent with your numbers.

Receipts, invoices, and accurate financial statements act as tools with which to handle the twists and turns of tax laws. Each step emphasizes the importance of maintaining a well-organized ledger, acting as a shield during the tax-filing process. Meticulous record keeping ensures a confident journey through the intricate aspects of tax compliance. This approach highlights the significance of attention to detail and a dedication to preserving accurate records, which are essential for surmounting the challenges posed by evolving tax requirements. Crafting a Paper Trail: Documenting Profits and Losses

Maintaining a clear record of your business' profits and losses through a meticulous paper trail is crucial. Begin by organizing transactions in a general ledger, whether by using accounting software or manual methods. Document your sales details and expenses, and reconcile bank statements regularly. Keep records of invoices, receipts, and sales orders, and categorize your expenses accurately. It's incredibly important to preserve copies of all financial documents, including purchase orders and payroll records. Freshbooks and Expensify have apps that allow you to scan receipts and keep them organized online.

Maintain a log of your assets and track their depreciation over time. Ensure that you consistently maintain a list of fixed assets as well. Keep important tax documents and regularly create financial statements. When utilizing accounting software, leverage the audit trail feature to monitor and trace any modifications made. Document all adjustments to financial records, and have a policy for keeping records to comply with the law. This thorough documentation not only ensures accurate financial reports—it also helps in audits and decision making, and it shows financial responsibility to stakeholders and regulators.

Self-Employment Tax Navigation

Employee owners and shareholders have certain tax obligations concerning self-employment, dividends, and capital gains tax, and being aware of them is the difference between smooth sailing or trouble waters come tax season.

Solo Tax Burdens: Mitigating Self-Employment Tax

Self-employment tax is paid by individuals who are owners of a company. S corporation shareholders or owners don't pay self-employment tax on the entire income generated by the business; structuring the business as an S corporation enables owners to minimize or avoid self-employment tax by receiving a combination of salary and dividends.

As compared to traditional employees, self-employed individuals bear the responsibility for both the employer and employee portions of Social Security and Medicare taxes on their wages, leading to an increased tax liability. By combining available deductions, business expenses, retirement plan contributions, and proper tax planning, those who are self-employed can reduce their tax burden. Plus, the dividends are not subject to these taxes.

Capital Gains and Dividends: Smarter Tax Handling

With an S corporation, capital gains and dividends are considered pass-through income. When the corporation realizes a capital gain from the sale of assets, shareholders report their share of the gain on their individual tax returns, with the tax treatment depending on the holding period.

S corporations do not issue dividends. Instead, shareholders receive their portion of profits through distributions, which are generally tax-free if they don't exceed the shareholder's basis (the percentage of the company that the shareholder owns). Shareholders may also receive ordinary income, such as salary or compensation, which is subject to individual income tax rates.

Maintaining accurate records of shareholder basis is crucial for determining the tax consequences of distributions. Special considerations may apply to built-in gains. Navigating the tax implications of capital gains and distributions in an S corporation requires careful attention to individual circumstances, and it often involves consulting with tax professionals to ensure compliance with tax laws.

Unlocking the Potential of S Corporation Tax Credits

S corporations use tax credits effectively to grow, stay competitive, and improve their overall financial well-being. To make the most of S corporation tax credits, you need to carefully explore available opportunities and use these credits wisely to cut down on your taxes.

Charting the Course for Tax Credits

Using available credits lowers tax bills, but it also encourages innovation and creates more jobs. As with any tax credit, a tax professional can ensure that you're following the rules, keeping proper records, and staying updated on rule changes.

Tailoring Tax Relief: Specific Credits for Your S Corp

Customizing tax relief for your S corporation involves identifying and leveraging specific credits that align with your business activities. Tailoring your approach to tax credits can optimize financial benefits and reduce overall tax liability. Some key credits for S corporations to consider include the Research and Development (R&D) Tax Credit, which rewards innovation and development efforts, and the Work Opportunity Tax Credit (WOTC), which encourages the hiring of employees from target groups.

Additionally, the Small Business Health Care Tax Credit supports businesses providing health insurance, while the Disabled Access Credit facilitates making business premises accessible. For those investing in energy efficiency, the Energy-Efficient Commercial Building Deduction and Investment Tax Credit (ITC) offer potential relief. Exploring these and other credits, aligning them with your business' specific activities, and staying informed about eligibility criteria can maximize the impact of tax relief for your S corporation. It's recommended that you seek professional advice to ensure compliance.

Alliances with Tax Professionals

Doing your research and having a compliance officer is great, but a tax professional whose sole job is to keep abreast of tax rules and changes can prove invaluable. Online forums are a great place to keep up with changes.[7]

The Value of Professional Expertise

Tax professionals serve as invaluable allies with their specialized knowledge of intricate tax laws and regulations. They can assist in optimizing tax outcomes through meticulous planning, identifying deductions, leveraging incentives, compliance assurance, cost savings, and efficient financial strategies. During complex transactions or audits, tax professionals provide essential support, ensuring that businesses navigate these challenges seamlessly.

When searching for a tax professional, choose one that specializes in taxes and S corporations. Make sure that they're a good match—they should have open lines of communication and a keen attention to detail, understand how your business works, and be able to effectively represent you with tax authorities.

Their guidance ensures compliance with ever-changing regulations and reduces the risk of errors in tax filings. By collaborating with tax advisors, businesses can implement proactive strategies, mitigate risks, and make informed financial decisions. This precision approach to tax planning is instrumental in achieving financial well-being, as well as maintaining a strategic edge in the competitive landscape.

Forecasting and Compliance for Shareholders

Shareholders benefit from forecasting by projecting their income, expenses, and potential tax obligations. This proactive approach allows for strategic planning, enabling shareholders to allocate resources efficiently and make informed financial decisions.

Quarter by Quarter: Planning for Estimated Tax Payments

Each quarter, taxpayers are required to make estimated payments toward their annual tax liability. Determining how much to pay involves estimating income, calculating tax obligations, and making timely payments to the IRS or other tax authorities. Quarterly payments ensure a steady and predictable allocation of funds for taxes, preventing financial stress during tax filing season.

Being organized and proactive enables taxpayers to adjust their estimated payments as income and expenses change throughout the year. This structured approach to tax planning promotes compliance with tax regulations, reducing the risk of underpayment penalties. Moreover, it empowers individuals and businesses to have more control over their cash flow and financial responsibilities throughout the year.

Confronting the IRS: Strategies for Audits and Inquiries

Facing an audit from the IRS can be a daunting prospect, but adopting a strategic approach can help you navigate the situation with ease.

First, stay calm and cooperative, and respond to inquiries promptly. Bring in a tax advisor or attorney to provide guidance. Review and understand the basis of the audit or inquiry, and know your rights. If you've maintained thorough and accurate records, you should be prepared to provide the IRS with what they need and prove that you're in compliance.

Exiting with Ease: The Sale of an S Corporation

Selling an S corporation requires careful planning to ensure a smooth transition that matches your financial goals. There are a number of factors to consider with this move, which we'll delve into below.

The Tax-Smart Exit: Planning for the Sale of Your S Corp

When you're gearing up to sell your S corporation, it's vital to dive into options that not only cut down on taxes but also boost your profits.

Often, you're faced with the decision of selling assets or stocks, each carrying its own set of tax implications.

It's not just about the numbers—it's also about aligning your unique financial goals. This involves working closely with professionals: your trusted tax experts, financial advisors, and legal professionals. They offer personalized advice, assist in decision making, and deftly navigate the intricacies of tax laws, ensuring a seamless and tax-efficient transition out of the S corporation.

Ultimately, envision a well-crafted plan that not only trims down your tax burdens but also sets you and your fellow shareholders on a path to enduring financial success.

Retirement Readiness: S Corp Strategies for Later Life

Embarking on the journey toward retirement as an S corporation owner involves some personalized moves to make sure that you're set for your golden years. First, you need to balance income and distribution. Ensure that you have enough to live on, and fund a qualified retirement account that meets IRS guidelines, such as a 401(k), 403(b), profit sharing, or Keogh (HR-10) plans.

As an employee of the S corporation, you're also required to pay Social Security tax, which you can draw from in your later years. Regularly review your portfolio to confirm that your investments are growing and continuing to align with your retirement goals.

Navigating State-by-State Tax Obligations

Tax obligations are dictated by the state where you incorporate and do business. Depending on where your organization is located, you're subject to the applicable requirements of that state, but sometimes gray areas and confusion exist.

Charting the State Tax Landscape: A Guide for S Corps

Earlier, we mentioned some of the best states in which to incorporate. Now let's talk about what happens when your business crosses state lines, as you may be obligated to pay taxes and follow regulations in multiple jurisdictions.

It's up to you and your meticulous record-keeping system to allocate the

correct funds to the correct jurisdiction. Each state or municipality may also have different incentives, filing requirements, and credits for federal taxes paid. When your company starts to branch out beyond your state or city, it's recommended that you consult a tax professional for assistance.

Regional Tax Tactics: Adapting to State-Level Obligations

Each state operates with unique tax policies, and S corporations need to tailor their approaches accordingly. Consider where you choose your home office strategically. Regional tax tactics involve continuous assessment, adaptation, and alignment with the unique tax environments of each state in which a business operates.

Tech-Forward Tax Compliance: Leveraging Software

In our digital age, there's no excuse for not being aware of what's required of you and taking advantage of the existing—and constantly improving—technology. There are a myriad of tech tools out there that can make tax compliance easier than ever before.

The Best Accounting Software for S Corps

The right accounting software can significantly streamline tax duties, and one top pick is QuickBooks. Its user-friendly interface and robust features make bookkeeping a breeze, helping S corps efficiently manage income, expenses, and payroll. Another contender is Xero, which offers cloud-based solutions that facilitate collaboration among team members and ensure real-time financial insights.

FreshBooks stands out for its simplicity, making it an excellent choice for smaller S corporations. Its invoicing and expense-tracking features simplify financial management. Wave Accounting, a free option, caters to budget-conscious S corps, providing core accounting functionalities without the price tag. Zoho Books is a versatile choice, integrating seamlessly with other business tools and offering comprehensive financial management capabilities.

Ultimately, the best accounting software for your S corporation depends on your specific needs and preferences, so explore these options to digitize and optimize your tax-related tasks.

Integrating Tech Tools

S corporations can leverage various tech tools to enhance tax compliance and overall financial management. For efficient tax filing, consider using tax preparation software such as TurboTax Business or H&R Block Business, both designed to navigate the complexities of business tax returns. Streamline expense tracking with tools such as Expensify or Receipt Bank, which automate the categorization of expenses and ensure accurate reporting. Payroll software like Gusto or ADP can automate payroll processing, including tax withholdings, which contributes to compliance with payroll tax regulations.

Implement electronic document management systems such as DocuWare or SharePoint for secure storage and easy retrieval of important tax-related documents. Gain in-depth insights into financial data with business intelligence tools like Tableau or Power BI, supporting strategic tax planning and decision-making. Tools such as Carta or Capdesk can assist in managing ownership, stock options, and equity matters for accurate reporting and compliance.

Cloud accounting platforms like Sage Intacct or NetSuite provide flexibility and enable real-time collaboration. Explore automated compliance monitoring tools such as ComplyRight or Thomson Reuters Checkpoint to stay updated on changes in tax laws that impact your S corporation. Streamline document processes with electronic signature platforms like DocuSign or DocHub, as they reduce paperwork and enhance efficiency.

Tax Implications of Employee Compensation

How an S corporation handles compensation and payroll affects how much tax is owed, so it's important to demystify the factors that can complicate things if you're not privy to their potential ramifications.

Decoding Compensation Taxes

Employee benefits like health insurance, retirement plans, and fringe benefits can have favorable tax treatment for both the employer and the employee. These benefits not only enhance employee satisfaction but also bring potential tax benefits.

However, it's important to be aware of the tax rules associated with each benefit to stay compliant and make the most of these advantages. Regularly staying informed about changes in tax laws and reviewing compensation strategies helps S corporations adapt and succeed in the ever-changing tax landscape. Essentially, decoding compensation taxes allows businesses to offer attractive benefits while being tax efficient.

Payroll Tax Prowess: Ensuring Accurate Filings and Payments

Nailing payroll tax means keeping precise records of employee wages, calculating tax withholdings correctly, and meeting filing deadlines. Using reliable payroll software can make these tasks easier. S corporation owners need to stay in the loop about changes in tax laws by following federal, state, and local tax requirements to avoid penalties. Regularly checking and auditing payroll records can catch mistakes early on. Make sure that payroll taxes are paid accurately and on time to avoid interest and penalties. Having a solid system in place, possibly with professional help, is crucial for an S corporation's financial health and compliance.

Navigating the Newest S Corp Tax Laws - 2024 & Beyond

S corporations must constantly stay informed about legislative changes and IRS guidance that can significantly impact their tax liabilities and compliance strategies. And 2024 brings in many developments for these entities. Staying current on these changes is about taking opportunities to optimize tax outcomes, manage operational risks, and position the corporation advantageously in a competitive market environment.

For S corporations, understanding these updates will help with strategic planning, defending against inadvertent non-compliance, and making decisions that align with both current and future tax obligations.

Understanding the IRS Rev. Proc. 2022-19: Simplifying Compliance for S Corporations

The IRS's issuance of Rev. Proc. 2022-19 marks a step toward simplifying compliance and providing relief for S corporations grappling with common compliance challenges. This procedural update brings clarity and flexibility, especially in areas where inadvertent errors or omissions could previously lead to disproportionate consequences.

Procedural Changes and Simplified Compliance Measures:

Rev. Proc. 2022-19 introduces streamlined procedures for addressing issues related to the S corporation election process, the one-class-of-stock requirement, and other inadvertent errors. For instance, it outlines a more straightforward approach for rectifying ineligible S corporation elections or terminations without resorting to the more cumbersome process of seeking private letter rulings. This reduces administrative burdens on S corporations and lowers the financial impact of obtaining such rulings.

Relief Provisions for Common Compliance Issues:

Rev. Proc. 2022-19 highlights its logical stance on the one-class-of-stock rule, which is a foundation of S corporation eligibility. The procedure acknowledges that certain arrangements or agreements might inadvertently create scenarios that seem to violate this rule. Under the new guidance, provided there is no principal purpose to bypass the requirement, such arrangements will not automatically disqualify an entity's S status.

Furthermore, the procedure offers a path for retroactively correcting non-identical governing provisions without the need for IRS intervention, as long as specific conditions are met. This includes consistent tax filing behavior and the lack of disproportionate distributions that could reflect on the integrity of the one-class-of-stock requirement.

These updates signify the IRS's recognition of S corporations' practical challenges and commitment to facilitating compliance through clearer guidelines and corrective measures. For S corporations, leveraging these provisions requires an understanding of the procedural changes and how they can effectively address past, present, and future compliance issues.

Changes in S Corporation Eligibility and Classification

There have been modifications in Section 1362 of the Internal Revenue Code for S corporations, which outlines the criteria for electing, revoking, or terminating S corporation status. These alterations significantly affect the corporate framework and the relationship dynamics among shareholders.

Section 1362(g) now imposes restrictions on S corporations whose election has been terminated, barring them from re-electing S corporation status before the fifth tax year after the year of termination without IRS consent. This change directs careful consideration by corporations before making any decision that could lead to the termination of their S status.

Moreover, **relief provisions** have been introduced for corporations that inadvertently fail to meet the eligibility criteria, either at the time of the election or subsequently. The need for a taxpayer to request a private letter ruling for relief, alongside the associated user fees, stresses the need for careful record-keeping and awareness of tax obligations.

The Impact of the Corporate Transparency Act and FinCEN Regulations on S Corporations

Recent federal court rulings have updated the Corporate Transparency Act (CTA) and its enforcement, prompting a pause by the Financial Crimes Enforcement Network (FinCEN). These developments affect S Corporations, especially concerning new reporting and transparency requirements.

The CTA aims to combat financial crimes by requiring businesses to report beneficial ownership information to FinCEN. However, the pause in enforcement and legal challenges have introduced uncertainty for S Corporations regarding their compliance obligations. S Corporations must stay informed about these changes, as the outcome of current legal proceedings could dictate new reporting requirements.

The Complexities of Passthrough Entity Taxation (PTET) Regimes

In response to the State and Local Tax (SALT) deduction cap introduced by the Tax Cuts and Jobs Act, several states have developed Passthrough Entity Taxation (PTET) regimes as a workaround. These regimes allow S Corporations to elect to pay state taxes at the entity level, circumventing the SALT cap and potentially reducing the tax burden on individual shareholders. However, PTET regimes vary significantly across states.

For S Corporations, these complexities involve a detailed analysis of each state's PTET rules, including eligibility criteria, tax rate implications, and the potential impact on shareholders' tax liabilities. Additionally, S Corporations must consider the interplay between state-level PTET elections and federal tax obligations, ensuring their tax strategy optimizes overall tax efficiency across jurisdictions.

Strategic considerations might include analyzing the benefits of a PTET election in each state of operation, understanding the implications for non-resident shareholders, and integrating state tax planning with overall business objectives. Given the evolving nature of PTET regimes and ongoing legislative changes, S Corporations should consult with tax professionals to understand these complexities effectively.

Recent IRS Guidance on Employee Retention Credits and its Effect on S Corporations

The Internal Revenue Service (IRS) further clarified the Employee Retention Credit (ERC) claims, stressing the necessity for businesses, including S Corporations, to adjust wage expenses accordingly. The ERC, designed to encourage employers to keep employees on their payroll during the COVID-19 pandemic, requires that wage expenses claimed for the credit must be reduced by the amount of the credit claimed. This adjustment is important for S Corporations as it directly affects the calculation of taxable income and potentially the distributions to shareholders.

The challenge for S Corporations lies in the timing and recognition of these adjustments, especially if ERC claims are processed after the filing of tax returns. Strategies to mitigate adverse tax implications include amending prior year returns to accurately reflect reduced wage expenses and considering the impact on shareholder allocations. S Corporations should carefully plan and consult with tax professionals to understand these requirements effectively and optimize their tax positions.

The Future of R&E Expenditure Capitalization

Section 174 of the Internal Revenue Code is undergoing significant changes, mandating the capitalization and amortization of Research & Experimentation (R&E) expenses starting from tax years beginning after December 31, 2021. This shift from immediate expensing to a more prolonged recovery period could considerably impact S Corporations.

S Corporations must now spread the deduction of R&E expenses over five years (or fifteen years for foreign research), altering cash flow projections and potentially increasing short-term taxable income. However, the possibility of legislative reversals or delays remains as discussions and proposals to modify or postpone these changes are ongoing. S Corporations should closely monitor legislative developments and consider current and future R&E expenditure treatment implications in their tax planning and financial modeling.

Preparing for the Future Tax Landscape

S Corporations must prioritize proactive tax planning and adaptability to regulatory changes. Staying informed and consulting with tax professionals is recommended to keep up with the tax code's complexities and optimize tax positions.

Key Takeaways

- Taxes depend on where your S corporation is set up and where it does business.

- Technology tools can make life easier.

- How a shareholder is compensated can make a big difference in how much taxes are owed.

- Compliance with tax deadlines is crucial to retaining your S corporation status.

Chapter 5

Bookkeeping Basics for S Corps

"The word accounting comes from the word accountability. If you are going to be rich, you need to be accountable for your money."
-**Robert T. Kiyosaki, Japanese-American businessman and author**

Why Accurate Bookkeeping is KEY (And How to Do It)

Proper and accurate bookkeeping is crucial for managing business finances. Its goals are to meet compliance requirements, make tax preparation easier, and offer insights into your company's financial health.

As long as you follow basic accounting rules and can generate the required reports, you can create a bookkeeping system that works for you. For some, this means using the latest technology; for others, it could look like paper ledgers and baskets of receipts. As your company grows—and especially if you enlist outside help for financial reporting—you'll want to create an easy-to-understand system that your entire company can follow.

And, a word of advice: Setting up a system in the beginning is much easier than playing catch-up with your books later.

Tips for Organizing Financial Documents

Whichever method you choose, it's important to be organized. You should always be able to, for example, find a particular receipt online or in a file cabinet in a short amount of time. **Here's how to achieve this:**

- Establish a filing system that's logical and intuitive to you and your accounting team. Common categories include income, expenses, taxes, contracts, and receipts.

- Separate business and personal expenses.

- Use digital tools such as Google Drive or Dropbox. These cloud-based tools allow easy access from multiple devices while keeping the documents secure.

- Scan and store receipts to minimize paper clutter.

- Organize bank statements, invoices, and time-sensitive documents by date.

- Label documents clearly with names, dates, and other relevant details.

- If you store items online, make sure that you backup your files.

- Store important documents in a secure place offsite so that they're protected in the event of fire or theft.

- Shred documents that are no longer required. Check the IRS rules to see which ones you need to keep.

Tracking Income and Expenses

Monitor all income and expenses efficiently by utilizing accounting

software, spreadsheets, or other financial management tools. These two categories are used on your income statement, so keeping records up-to-date will give you a clear picture of your company's financial health.

Get into the habit of recording sales and revenue, such as service fees or product sales, as they occur. Invoice clients or customers promptly, and then follow up so that they adhere to the payment terms and due dates.

Categorize and track expenses like utilities, rent, office supplies, travel, and employee wages. All expenses should be supported by documentation, such as purchase orders or receipts. Automate recurring expenses to reduce the risk of missing payments. Label and track expenses that are tax deductible, such as meals, travel, and home office expenses.

Create regular financial reports and review them carefully. Balance sheets, income statements, and statements outlining cash flow provide insights into your company's financial performance.

Software and Tools for Bookkeeping

Software like QuickBooks, Wave, Xero, and Zoho can help ease bookkeeping tasks. Some features to look for when choosing software are invoice and expense tracking, bank reconciliation, payroll processing, financial reporting, online invoicing and billing, job costing, time tracking, inventory management, and tax planning tools.

While one piece of software might not meet all these needs, some of them come very close. Choose the best one for your current requirements, and then add programs as you grow. An accountant or bookkeeping specialist is a great resource to get your system set up.

Setting Up A Chart of Accounts

A chart of accounts provides a structured framework for recording and reporting financial information. It's customizable based on the specific needs and structure of your company, so as your business evolves, so will the chart of accounts.

Each category has a numerical code to make it easier to reference, and each account has a descriptive title. Accounts are broken down into different types to help organize your financial information for reporting and analysis. Also, each account can have multiple sub-accounts.

The following is a sample chart of accounts:

- 1000-1999 Assets

  o 1100 Cash

  o 1200 Accounts Receivable

  o 1300 Inventory

- 2000-2999 Liabilities

  o Accounts Payable

  o Loans Payable

- 3000-3999 Equity

- o   3100 Owner's Equity

- 4000-4999 Revenue

  - o   4100 Sales - Product A

  - o   4200 Sales - Product B

- 5000-5999 Cost of Goods Sold (COGS)

  - o   5100 COGS - Product A

  - o   5200 COGS - Product B

- 6000-6999 Operating Expenses

  - o   6100 Rent

  - o   6200 Utilities

  - o   6300 Advertising

Managing Invoices and Receipts

Invoices are sent to a customer when they owe you money for a good or service you've provided. Most accounting software can send and track invoices, and they can even send reminders if your customers miss their due date.

A smart practice is to send invoices as soon as you deliver a good or service and set favorable (to you) payment terms. Specify a due date and any applicable late fees. You can maintain order with sequential invoice numbers and provide various payment options to encourage timely payments. Always keep track of outstanding balances and follow up—after all, your cash flow depends on it.

Receipts track expenses, and lost receipts are detrimental to your bottom line. Instead of relying on slips of paper that are easily misplaced, opt for electronic receipts—or at the very least scan them into a device the first chance you get. Once they're online, assign each expense a category and enter them into your accounting software.

How to Categorize Transactions

Armed with your chart of accounts, it should now be straightforward to categorize transactions. Ask yourself whether it's an income or an expense, and then assign it a category.

Tracking Business Mileage and Expenses

When employees are required to travel for their job for client meetings, deliveries, or travel between work locations, the company can claim this as an expense. Maintain a mileage log that includes the date of the trip, the starting and ending locations, the purpose of the trip, and the odometer reading of the vehicle. Apps such as MileIQ, TripLog, or Everlance will simplify this.

For other business expenses—such as meals, lodging, fuel, parking, or tolls—collect receipts. If the employee uses a business credit card, you can use the card statement to simplify tracking. Using your chart of accounts, assign each type of expense a category. If the employee is paid for meals or other incidental expenses, you can pay them a per diem (a set amount per day) instead of detailed receipts.

Detailed expense tracking not only ensures that employees are reimbursed for business expenses that they initially pay out of their own pocket, but it also enables you to track how much it actually costs to do business and allows accurate deductions on tax returns.

Handling Payroll and Employee Records

If you draw a salary or have employees, you need to ensure accurate compensation, follow labor laws, and maintain employee information. The easiest way to do this is by using payroll software such as Gusto, ADP, or QuickBooks Payroll. Other payroll-related factors to consider include when to pay employees, taxes that need to be withheld, and whether employees are exempt or non-exempt based on labor laws.

Your company is also required to keep a file for each employee with essential documents such as resumes, offer letters, eligibility paperwork, employee contracts, performance reviews, contact details, emergency contacts, and attendance. You can also track training and development, benefits, and leaves of absence.

Be aware, however, that all this information is confidential and should be securely stored.

Reconciling Financial Statements

To maintain financial integrity, you must compare your accounting records with your bank statements. Regularly reconciling your accounts enables you to promptly identify and address any discrepancies.

To reconcile your accounts, follow these steps:

- Compare beginning balances.

- Match transactions.

- Identify any differences.

- Subtract outstanding checks and make adjustments for any outstanding deposits.

- Check for bank errors.

- Ensure that you end up with the same ending balance as the bank and can account for any differences.

Managing Vendor and Supplier Accounts

Managing these accounts can help you control costs, manage cash flow, build positive relationships, ensure a stable supply chain, reduce risks, maintain contractual compliance, help you operate efficiently, and enable you to plan for the future.

You can manage vendor and supplier accounts through an effective management system, where contact information, payment terms, contract details, and all other information are easily accessible. When contracts come to an end, evaluate how the relationship is working, and see if you can negotiate better payment terms, discounts, and volume purchases. Compare your current contract with other vendors, and use purchase orders to ensure consistency and transparency.

Handling Sales Tax and Use Tax

Sales tax is a consumption tax levied by the government on the sale of goods and services. In contrast, use tax is typically imposed on the use, storage, or consumption of tangible personal property that wasn't subject to taxation at the time of purchase.

Recognize what taxes you're required to collect and where to remit, which depends on your location and may include state, county, and municipal taxes. Sales tax is typically collected at the point of sale. Tax calculation software can automatically add taxes based on the customer's location and the type of product or service.

In cases where a customer is exempt from sales tax, they're required to provide a certificate as proof of exemption. You'll then flag their account to ensure that you don't charge them. Sales tax must be set to the proper taxing authorities according to their schedule. Keep in mind that late payments can result in interest or penalties.

Types of taxes and rates can change, so keep on top of these with updates to your software and invoicing policies. As taxes are often complicated, consult a tax attorney or professional to ensure that you're in compliance. The taxing authority may be a decent source of information as well.

Keeping Track of Shareholder Distributions

Shareholder distributions can take various forms, including dividends, stock buybacks, and other forms of payments made to the owners of a company. Establish clear and documented policies regarding how and when shareholder distributions will be made. In addition, set up an accounting system to precisely record and monitor shareholder distributions.

Keep detailed records of each shareholder distribution, including the date, amount, form of distribution (cash, stock, etc.), and the names of shareholders receiving the distribution. If your company issues dividends, ensure that they're formally declared by the board of directors. This declaration should specify the amount, record date, and payment date. If your company engages in stock buybacks, document each transaction, including the number of shares repurchased, the price paid per share, and the total cost.

Maintain transparent communication with shareholders by keeping them informed about upcoming distributions, whether in the form of dividends or stock buybacks. Keep shareholder records up to date, especially if there are changes in ownership or if new shareholders are added.

Managing Equity Accounts

Equity represents the ownership interest of shareholders in the company, and it's crucial to keep accurate records to ensure transparency, compliance, and effective decision making. Familiarize yourself with the different components of equity, including stock, additional paid-in capital, retained earnings, and other comprehensive income. Understand the company's equity structure, including the number of shares outstanding, types of shares, and any special rights or preferences associated with the class of shares.

Document the issuance of new shares, whether through stock offerings, employee stock options, convertible securities, or other means. This includes recording the number of shares issued, the issuance date, and the consideration received. If your company issues dividends, document the declaration, record, and payment dates. Clearly distinguish between dividends and distributions.

Ensure precise representation of equity transactions in the company's financial statements, including the balance sheet, statement of changes in equity, and relevant footnotes. Also make sure that all equity transactions comply with legal and regulatory requirements.

Recording Asset Acquisitions and Depreciation

Upon acquiring a new asset, retain all pertinent documentation, including purchase orders, invoices, contracts, and payment receipts.

Establish specific asset accounts on your balance sheet for the acquired assets. This may include categories like machinery, equipment, vehicles, or buildings. Assign unique numbers or identification codes to each acquired asset.

Decide on the depreciation method you'll use to allocate the cost of the asset over its useful life, and then select the appropriate depreciation schedule based on the chosen method. Common schedules include monthly, quarterly, or annually.

Check and update your financial records regularly. If an asset's value changes or if you use a new depreciation method, review and adjust the calculations. When selling or disposing of an asset early, make necessary journal entries to remove its cost and depreciation from your financial statements.

For example, let's suppose that you purchased a piece of equipment for $50,000, with an estimated useful life of 10 years and no residual value. You use straight-line depreciation, so each year, you would depreciate the equipment by $5,000 ($50,000/10 years). After three years, the accumulated depreciation would be $15,000 (3 years x $5,000 per year).

Now, let's say that the piece of equipment needs replacement after three years, and you acquire a new one for $45,000.

Book Value of the old equipment after three years: $50,000 (original cost) - $15,000 (accumulated depreciation) = $35,000. Determine the Gain or Loss: Cost of the new equipment ($45,000) - Book Value of the old equipment ($35,000). In this case, it's a gain of $10,000.

Adjust Depreciation for the New Equipment: The cost of the new equipment is $45,000, but since there's a gain, you adjust it: $45,000 -

$10,000 (gain) = $35,000. The remaining useful life is still seven years (10 years - three years).

Recording Journal Entries:

- Debit Accumulated Depreciation (to remove the old equipment's accumulated depreciation)

- Debit Loss on Disposal (if it's a loss) or Credit Gain on Disposal (if it's a gain)

- Debit Equipment (new) for $35,000

- Credit Equipment (old) for $35,000

Impact on Financial Statements: The gain of $10,000 will be included in the income statement. The new equipment will be listed on the balance sheet at its adjusted cost of $35,000.

Budgeting for Bookkeeping Expenses

When first starting out, you may be able to handle the bookkeeping tasks for your own business on your own. There are clear benefits to this—the more you know how to do it, the better you'll understand your financial situation. But as your business grows and becomes more complex, you might require more comprehensive bookkeeping services. **There are a few options to consider:**

- You can hire a bookkeeper to handle some tasks, such as transaction recording, bank reconciliation, accounts payable and receivable management, financial reporting, and compliance duties.

- Consider hiring someone to provide bookkeeping services on a daily, weekly, or monthly basis. Or perhaps you simply require a periodic review.

- You could hire someone on a contract basis or a full-time employee.

- You could also rely on software to make your life easier.

Consider your budget and the amount of work that you'd like to outsource. Anticipate any additional costs related to bookkeeping, such as training expenses for in-house staff, software upgrades, or any compliance-related costs. Anticipate any additional costs related to bookkeeping, like training expenses for in-house staff, software upgrades, or any compliance-related costs.

How to Automate Bookkeeping Tasks

If your operation is small and you'd like to keep your bookkeeping as efficient as possible, look for ways to automate certain tasks. Choose an accounting software that meets the needs of your business and integrates with your bank accounts and credit cards. Create rules that'll allow the system to automatically categorize transactions.

Streamline invoicing and payments by automating the process. Implement automatic reminders for clients with overdue invoices. Additionally, automate payroll (as long as the information remains consistent from week to week). If you scan receipts into your system, some software will automatically categorize expenses. Many software packages will also generate required reports with the click of a button.

Documenting Financial Processes and Procedures

Document your processes for consistent and efficient financial management. This ensures a seamless transition between workers, as well as creates a clear understanding of how things work. Create documents for budgeting, invoicing, payroll, financial reporting, expense management, and any other process you perform regularly.

To create a document, write down the step-by-step process. You can use flow charts, screenshots, or written step-by-step instructions. Outline the tasks, responsibilities, and actions required at each stage. Incorporate essential internal controls and checks within your financial processes to prevent errors, fraud, or other financial irregularities. Clearly outline the software and tools employed for each process, along with detailed instructions on their usage. And then make sure that you review the documentation regularly to ensure that the processes are up to date.

Dealing with Bookkeeping Errors and Discrepancies

Quickly find and fix errors to ensure that your financial information is reliable. Common mistakes can include mathematical, data-entry, transposition, and categorization errors. Catching them before they become major headaches is key.

Regular reconciliations can identify discrepancies between your financial records and internal statements. Make a record of the error and determine the impact. Determine what caused the error—your data entry, the bank, or a software glitch are the most common factors. Do what you can to correct the error by adjusting journal entries or correcting the category. Also, learn what you can do to prevent the errors in the future, perhaps by adding more robust controls.

Acknowledge that mistakes can occur, and then take proactive measures to prevent them from happening again.

When to Bring in a Bookkeeper/Accountant to Help

Bringing in an expert (even if it's just for a short time) can provide peace of mind and save countless hours of figuring it all out yourself. **Here's when to ask for advice:**

- When launching your business. Consider seeking the assistance of a bookkeeper or accountant to help establish a system that you can subsequently manage independently.

- During periods of expansion or rapid growth. A professional can pick up the slack to ensure that you don't fall behind.

- When faced with complex transactions, such as mergers, acquisitions, or large investments.

- During tax season, when financial reports are due, or if you're targeted for an audit.

- Anytime you need extra help.

Rather than struggle, add a cushion to your budget to hire an expert when you need it. Check out the National Association of Certified Public Bookkeepers for free resources.[10]

Key Takeaways

- A well-thought-out accounting system can save tremendous time in present and future financial tasks.

- Accounting software and tools can automate basic bookkeeping tasks.

- Engaging the services of a professional bookkeeper or accountant can provide valuable assistance with intricate accounting functions.

- Setting up a chart of accounts can help keep track of every detail and aid in forecasting and budgeting.

- Reconciling financial statements will catch errors and keep you on track.

Chapter 6

Mastering Payroll and People in S Corporations: The Human Element

"Employees are a company's greatest asset—they're your competitive advantage. You want to attract and retain the best; provide them with encouragement, stimulus, and make them feel that they are an integral part of the company's mission."
-Anne M. Mulcahy, former chairperson and CEO of Xerox

Business isn't just about number crunching and selling widgets. In fact, that's far from the case. As you grow your S corporation, you'll generally need to take on employees as well, and that also means taking on another host of responsibilities. Correctly managing the legal aspects of this, while also managing the human element, is key. Being aware of your employees' emotions, key traits, and their fit within the team is essential, as well as knowing when it's time to expand, maintain, or "clean house." This includes being able to have the tough conversations, such as when the time comes to let an employee go. Let's explore this area of managing your business, starting with the payroll and legal side of things. (Some of this information has been covered previously, but should be examined again within the context of human relations.)

Payroll Processing for S Corporations

Managing payroll for S corporations involves careful attention to legal and tax compliance, especially considering the unique relationship between shareholders and the corporation. Staying informed about changes in tax laws and seeking professional advice can help you to navigate payroll processing successfully.

S corporation employees, who are also shareholders, must be paid reasonable compensation for the services they provide. The IRS scrutinizes S corporations that pay unreasonably low salaries to shareholders as a way to minimize payroll taxes. Determining a reasonable salary involves considering factors such as industry standards, job responsibilities, and the financial health of the corporation.

Employee Benefits and Compensation

You may choose to provide your employees with various benefits and retirement plans, and these contributions can have tax advantages for both the corporation and the employees. Common options include 401(k) plans and health savings accounts (HSAs).

Apart from retirement plans and HSAs, S corporations have the flexibility to provide a range of additional employee benefits, including health insurance, dental and vision coverage, life insurance, disability insurance, and more. Some benefits may be provided on a pre-tax basis, reducing employees' taxable income and providing tax advantages.

Ensure that your employee benefits and retirement plans comply with relevant regulations, including the Employee Retirement Income Security Act (ERISA) and the Internal Revenue Code.

Compliance with Labor Laws

In addition to federal regulations, you need to comply with state and local payroll tax regulations as well. Each jurisdiction may have its own rules regarding income tax withholding, unemployment taxes, and other payroll-related matters. The US Government outlines federal labor laws online at www.usa.gov/labor-laws.[11]

You're required to provide Form W-2 to each employee, detailing their annual compensation, taxes withheld, and other relevant information. Employees need this form when filing their personal tax returns.

The following are some of the labor laws that an S corporation must comply with:

- Fair Labor Standards Act (FLSA): addresses minimum wage and overtime requirements

- Occupational Safety and Health Act (OSHA): ensures a safe work environment and the health of its employees while on the job

- Family and Medical Leave Act (FMLA): covers unpaid leave in the event of qualifying family or medical reasons

- Equal Employment Opportunity Commission Laws (EEOC): includes Title VII of the Civil Rights Act, the Americans with Disabilities Act (ADA), and the Age Discrimination in Employment Act (ADEA), all of which prohibit forms of discrimination based on race, religion, color, sex, disability, and age

- National Labor Relations Act (NLRA): covers the establishment of labor unions

Employee Classification and Exempt vs. Non-Exempt

As mentioned previously, S corporations typically have both shareholders and non-shareholder employees. Shareholders who provide work for the corporation are employees, and they receive wages and are subject to payroll taxes.

Employees can be classified in several ways:

- Full Time: those who typically work 40 hours per week

- Part Time: those who work fewer than 40 hours per week (and may not qualify for benefits)

- Temporary or Seasonal: those who work on a limited basis

- Salaried vs. Hourly: based on whether employees are paid a set amount or on a per-hour basis.

Independent contractors, interns, or consultants are not employees, and they're often not paid through the same payroll processes as regular employees.

Exempt employees are generally excluded from receiving overtime pay, and this is because they meet certain criteria such as earning a minimum salary or performing exempt job duties. Employees classified as non-exempt are eligible for overtime compensation for hours worked beyond the regular workweek.

Setting up Payroll Software and Systems

Utilizing software and systems to manage payroll is an efficient way to manage employee compensation, taxes, and other payroll tasks. Research payroll software and choose the right one for you based on your business' size, budget, and needs. Consider features such as tax compliance, direct deposit capabilities, reporting options, and integration with other business systems.

Establish clear policies regarding timekeeping, overtime, paid time off (PTO), and other relevant payroll matters, and input these policies into the payroll system to automate calculations. Enter employee deduction details, including health insurance premiums, retirement contributions, and additional benefits. If you offer direct deposit, set up the necessary bank information securely within the payroll system. Also, ensure that your payroll system is set up to automatically calculate and deduct the correct amount of taxes, including Social Security, Medicare, and income tax.

Retirement Plans and Contributions

S corporations have the flexibility to adopt various retirement plans, and the contributions made to these plans can offer numerous tax advantages. **There are several options to choose from:**

- Individual Retirements Accounts (IRAs): owners and employees can contribute to traditional or Roth IRAs

- Simplified Employee Pension (SEP) IRA: contributions are tax deductible and are based on a percentage of employee compensation.

- 401(k) Plans: contributions are made by both the employee and employer.

- Simple IRA: employees contribute through salary deferrals, and employers are required to make either non-elective or matching contributions.

Handling Payroll Deductions

Deductions are amounts withheld from employees' paychecks for various purposes such as taxes, benefits, and other voluntary contributions. Deductions for Social Security, Medicare, and income taxes are mandatory. Some are per individual and mandated by law, such as court-ordered garnishments, child support payments, or creditor judgments. Voluntary deductions include health insurance premiums, retirement plan contributions, and charitable contributions.

Collect necessary information from employees, such as tax withholding forms, benefit enrollment forms, and any other relevant documentation. Determine the appropriate amount to withhold for federal and state income tax, Medicare, and Social Security based on the information provided by employees. Ensure that your payroll software captures correct taxes and withdrawal amounts, and monitor employee changes that could affect payroll deductions.

Managing Employee Time and Attendance

Proper tracking and recording of hours worked by employees ensures accurate payroll processing, adherence to labor laws, and efficient allocation of resources. You might, for example, choose a way for employees to clock in/clock-out. Automated time-tracking solutions minimize errors and streamline the payment process.

Establish and communicate the standard work hours, break policies, and any overtime rules to employees, and ensure that these rules comply with labor laws. Your payroll system can track these items.

Even if your employees are salaried, they should still meet the expectations set forth regarding paid time off, sick leave, schedules, and so on.

Recruiting and Onboarding Employees

Effective recruitment ensures that you're attracting the right talent, while onboarding lays the foundation for a new employee's success in the company. To find the right candidates, create compelling job descriptions and well-defined job requirements. Use a variety of recruitment channels, including employee referrals. Ensure that candidates aren't just knowledgeable but are also compatible with your company's culture. Here's an easy tip, especially if you run a remote company: Conduct "qualifying" interviews, which are short, five- to 10-minute phone calls in which you chat with the employee and make sure that they're on board with everything as it relates to the job. You can also use these calls to screen out those who wouldn't be a good fit, and schedule in longer video or in-person interviews with those who seem the most promising.

Once employees are hired, create an onboarding process that sets them up for success, including training schedules, introductions to team members, and knowledge about the company. In addition, make certain that they're well-equipped with technology and know where to go for answers to questions. Another helpful tip is to record employee training materials. This allows you to systemize the process by simply equipping new employees with the recorded training content. For example, if you have a sales script you want them to memorize, record yourself going through the script with a new employee, and possibly even include and break down some of that employee's live calls or sales call roleplays. You can then use the recording for all new employees during the onboarding process going forward.

Investing in solid recruiting and onboarding processes helps companies bring in great talent, establish clear expectations, and smoothly integrate new employees into the company culture. This leads to happier employees, better retention, and overall success for your organization.

Performance Reviews and Appraisals

These performance measurement tools provide a structured way to assess employees' contributions while setting expectations and guiding professional development. While it's traditional to evaluate an employee on a yearly basis to determine whether they're eligible for a raise or promotion, it's highly recommended that you provide more consistent and ongoing feedback. This will allow you to set goals together based on the objectives of the company. Document performance and gather feedback from peers to provide a holistic perspective of how an employee is performing.

Use appraisals to provide constructive feedback, recognize achievements, set future goals, and discuss career development. Document future plans, and always follow up on expectations.

Regular performance reviews help organizations improve, guide employees in their growth, and connect individual efforts to the company's goals. Giving helpful feedback regularly boosts employee engagement and plays a pivotal role in the overall success of the organization. It's also a good idea to conduct a one-on-one quarterly check-in with each employee. This allows you to gauge where they're at mentally and how they're doing within their role, while also exposing any issues that you may not have been aware of. It enables you to address those issues before they become problematic.

Employee Termination and Severance

When an employment relationship ends, it's crucial to handle the process with care and ensure fair treatment. Things tend to go much smoother if there's a well-documented reason for termination. Focus on job-related factors and avoid personal attacks. Also, it's of vital importance to follow established company policies and labor laws.

Show empathy, offer support, and allow employees to collect their personal belongings and return company property. For terminations that are for financial reasons especially, you might offer a severance package based on the employee's years of service. This may include salary compensation, healthcare coverage, and/or retirement benefits. Ensure that you comply with any contractual agreements or legal obligations.

Workplace Safety and Compliance

Safety regulations and legal requirements protect employees and assist organizations in steering clear of legal issues. Potential hazards might include risk of physical danger (from equipment or wet floors), ergonomic concerns (from sitting at a desk for hours), and any other factor that could compromise employee safety. Use of safety equipment, training on what constitutes a safe work environment, and emergency response plans can be put in place to create awareness.

Ensure that you comply with applicable employment laws, regulations, and industry standards. Implement policies that protect employees' physical well-being, and provide reasonable accommodations required by the law. Write down all policies in an employee handbook and make sure that all employees receive proper training.

Handling Employee Disputes and Grievances

Addressing conflicts fairly and promptly helps uphold a positive work environment while promoting employee satisfaction. Encourage open communication and enlist the help of a mediator well before any conflicts escalate. If and when conflicts do occur, however, listen to all sides of the story and keep detailed documentation.

Having a clear grievance process in place, outlining the steps that employees should follow during disputes, is always advisable. In addition, provide conflict resolution training to both employees and managers. Learn from any conflicts that arise in the workplace, and use them to improve communication in the future.

Employee Training and Development

For your company to grow, you need employees who'll develop along with the goals of the business. This is achieved by enhancing employees' skills, knowledge, and abilities with different training methods, which can include online courses, job training, or mentorship programs. Sit down with each employee and determine their goals and how they relate to the company. Create individual development plans and offer skill-building opportunities.

The future leaders of your company are built from within, and so your focus should be on developing employees who are interested in growing into a larger role. If employees aren't interested in leadership positions, find out what their goals are and do your best to nurture them.

Dealing with Payroll Audits and Compliance Issues

Audits ensure accurate financial reporting and adherence regarding legal issues. To perform a payroll audit, gather documentation, including timesheets, pay stubs, tax forms, and employee records. Examine your payroll processes, diligently checking them for accuracy and compliance. If you discover errors, evaluate where they originated and whether you need to take corrective action. Internal audits exist to catch and correct errors before they amplify.

To ensure that you're in compliance with all regulations, document and follow policies related to overtime, paid time off, and benefits. Make sure that you're reviewing your processes and policies regularly to ensure timely and accurate submission to government agencies.

Remote and Virtual Team Management

Today's ever-evolving work environment means that you're able to offer employees a choice between remote work and working from the office (if the needs of the business allow it). Virtual options are often favorable to employees, as it allows them to work away from distractions and with more flexible work hours, but there can be challenges when it comes to making sure that all employees are on the same page. To mitigate this, set up project management tools for meetings and collaboration, and establish clear workload expectations. Frequently communicate with employees to confirm (and encourage) their productivity, and ensure that they have the tools necessary to carry out their tasks effectively.

Organize virtual team activities to strengthen team bonds, which could include virtual happy hours, collaborative projects, or online activities that extend beyond work tasks. Remote work can sometimes cause feelings of isolation, so it's essential to maintain open lines of communication. You can also take advantage of a tracking tool like Teramind, which allows you to remote-view employees' computers, as well as take control of their screen virtually. This can be especially helpful during training, but ensure that you have a fully transparent privacy policy in place that you and your employees sign off on.

Balancing Employee Rights and Employer Responsibilities

Balancing the workplace involves respecting employee rights like equal opportunities and fair pay, alongside fulfilling employer duties such as legal compliance and creating a safe environment. Employees should have clear policies and privacy protection, as well as ample opportunities to provide feedback.

One of your main priorities is to ensure safety, fair compensation, and professional growth. Promoting open communication, involving employees, and providing ongoing training are key to maintaining a positive and fair workplace. The aim is to create an environment where both employees' rights and your own responsibilities are upheld and exist in tandem.

Employee Retention and Engagement Strategies

How do you build a workplace where everyone feels valued and excited to contribute? By making the environment a great fit for your employees and creating a sense of connection. Beyond providing fair pay, acknowledge the unique contributions that each person brings to the team. The growth of your employees matters, so always explore opportunities for learning and advancement that align with their skills and interests.

Create a sense of community by encouraging open conversations about goals and how everyone can work together. Team activities, open-sharing, and celebrating successes are great ways of promoting and fostering engagement. Employees also enjoy feeling challenged and fulfilled, so create an environment where learning and participation is encouraged. In addition, consider adding some wellness programs, as they create a sense of balance for your employees.

As an employer, you can offer programs that cultivate fulfillment and create an environment where all employees have the opportunity to engage. Encourage employees to provide feedback on what will make the workplace one where they enjoy being—and one where they want to remain.

Legal and Regulatory Considerations

It's a given that ethical organizations must follow laws and regulations. This involves understanding and complying with local, state, and federal laws, creating clear contracts with legal advice, protecting intellectual property, and prioritizing data privacy. Compliance also extends to industry-specific rules, environmental standards, and consumer protection laws.

Financial regulations and health and safety standards are additional considerations. To address these challenges, seek legal advice, conduct regular audits, provide ongoing employee training, stay adaptable to changes, and maintain detailed documentation.

Employee Productivity and Motivation

Creating a thriving workplace involves making sure that employees are both productive and motivated. Start by setting clear goals and providing the tools needed for tasks, and also provide guidance on how team members can manage their time effectively. And remember—recognizing achievements will do wonders when it comes to boosting morale.

To foster motivation, connect tasks to the overall purpose of the organization and offer opportunities for growth. You can do this by fostering an inclusive culture, giving regular feedback, and encouraging all employees to prioritize well-being.

Balance is achieved by recognizing individual strengths, encouraging teamwork, and aligning goals with the organization's objectives. By doing these things, your S corporation can create a positive environment where employees work productively and are motivated to contribute their best. If you notice that a particular employee's productivity has decreased, sit down with them to see exactly what's going on, and help them identify ways to correct and work through it. The employee will appreciate you taking the time to hear them out, and just doing this alone goes a long way in making them feel important and valued. Here's an example. Years ago at one of our companies, there was a new employee who'd relocated for their position. He discovered that his new apartment was infested with cockroaches soon after he moved in, which was understandably stressful.

As his management team, we listened as he told us about his frustrating circumstances and helped him fix the situation. We put him in contact with a real estate lawyer and helped set him up in a new apartment. It only took us a short amount of time, but it made a world of difference to this employee. It's no surprise to us that he still works for our company years later. However, you don't always need to take a direct hand in fixing the employee's problem. Sometimes it's sufficient to simply sit with them and discuss potential solutions, and this will do wonders for both you and the employee in terms of being on the same page and moving toward a resolution.

Compensation Strategies for Different Industries

Compensation packages can vary according to your S corporation's industry. **The following are some guidelines and suggestions:**

- Technology and IT: Start with a competitive strategy based on talent, then add performance-based bonuses tied to the project or individual's success. Offer stock options or equity for a long-term commitment, and provide professional development opportunities to keep up with the latest technology.

- Healthcare: Begin with a competitive base pay and then add shift differentials, a comprehensive benefits package, and student loan repayment programs.

- Manufacturing: Compensation is generally based on an hourly wage, plus overtime pay. You might choose to offer incentives if employees follow safe practices.

- Finance and Banking: Offer competitive base salaries plus bonuses for peak performers, profit-sharing programs that tie bonuses to the company's financial success, and educational assistance programs to keep up on certifications or to pursue advanced degrees.

- Retail: Wages are often hourly or based on sales, but you can also add employee discounts, recognition programs for exceptional customer service, and flexible scheduling.

How to Create a Positive Workplace Culture

A positive culture in the workplace is crucial for happy employees and the overall success of your S corporation. It'll look different for each organization, but start by defining and communicating core values that align with the company's mission. Culture starts from the top, and so as a leader, you need to set a positive example and encourage open communication.

Key Takeaways

- Employees are a key component to your success, so pay careful attention to compensation, training, benefits, and retention.

- Happy employees are successful employees, and retention depends on compensation, benefits, and a positive work environment.

- A strong and productive workforce relies on recruiting employees that mesh with your company's culture and mission.

- Compensation packages can include carefully crafted remote work opportunities.

- Employers are ultimately responsible for following applicable laws and ensuring a safe work environment.

- Payroll audits ensure compliance with regulations, as well as accurate compensation packages.

By the way, to manage employees correctly, it helps to be an expert in the art of negotiation. This allows you to have the tough conversations necessary.

We show you how to become an expert in negotiation in our Negotiation Mastery Cheat Sheet, and you can get it free as part of your 7-Figure Business Toolkit. Click here to download it: llclegend.com/llc-s-corp-bonus

Chapter 7

Scaling Your S Corp to the Next Level

"The only strategy that is guaranteed to fail is not taking risks."
-Mark Zuckerberg, CEO of Meta

As your S corporation evolves and becomes more stable, the natural next step is to explore avenues for growth and expansion. This chapter will guide you through various strategies and considerations for scaling your S corporation to the next level.

Identifying Growth Opportunities and Markets

To grow your S corporation, you need a smart plan based on solid research and the ability to adapt. Start by studying the market to find new trends, what customers want, and any special markets you might be able to serve. Next, diversify your products or services and create new ones by carefully examining what you currently offer and what the market needs. Be innovative to differentiate yourself from the competition. Introduce new products or services carefully, and always be ready to adapt as the market changes. This way, your S corporation can stay flexible and achieve success in the business world.

If you create products, you could create new ones. If you offer services, you could add to them. If you do business in Texas, you could expand your reach to other states. Networking is a great way to explore new opportunities, and a great resource to start with is BNI (Business Networking International).[14]

Diversification and New Product Development

Diversifying your product or service offerings can be a key driver of growth. Look into different possibilities and create products or services that go well with what you already provide. In this way, you can meet a wider range of customer needs and attract more people to your business. Diversifying your offerings is a strategy that can drive growth and make your business more versatile.

Consider this example: Coca-Cola is an international company, and the formula for their famous soft drink has changed often over the years (remember New Coke?). Then, of course, there's Diet Coke and all the other flavors that belong to the brand. Each one of these started as a concept and ended up creating enormous hype and brand recognition.

Let's look at a smaller example—the Beast Dating Coaching Program. This business started off with one goal: to help men find their life partners. The concept worked well, bringing in a steady stream of new clients each month (typically professionally successful men with a desire to get married).

A few years into the business, owners Dave and David spotted an opportunity to expand. Most men in the program would organize a photoshoot and receive professional photos for their dating profiles so that they could attract more dates and have a better chance of meeting their potential partner. The problem, however, was that these men had a hard time finding photographers who knew what they were doing. While the photographers took good-quality photos, they weren't exactly what was needed to succeed and stand out in a sea of other men on the dating apps. Dave and David saw an opportunity here: Why not solve this problem *within* their business?

They teamed up with a local photographer in Austin, Texas and trained him on exactly how to take great dating app photos for men. From there, they launched their new service, Beast Photos, specifically geared toward getting great dating app profile shots. Not only did this lead to more sales from current clients who wanted to fly down for their photoshoot, but it also expanded the company's reach to men who didn't necessarily want dating coaching but only wanted to improve their dating profile.

This helped Dave and David to create a profitable new sector of their business, which they could then scale up even more. So for your S corporation, ask yourself this: Are there any adjacent problems that my customers deal with? Is there an additional service that would make sense for me to offer to help them solve it?

Strategic Partnerships and Alliances

Forming partnerships with other businesses is a smart strategy for growth. Collaborating opens up new markets, and it brings in technologies and resources that might be hard to access on your own. Partnerships are a way to access a larger customer base and boost revenue, and they can also help you stay competitive by introducing innovative technologies.

Sharing resources with partners leads to cost savings and efficiency—it's a way to share risks, especially when entering new markets. Learning from each other and combining skills can lead to mutual benefits. Regular evaluation and clear communication are key to successful partnerships, and they provide the flexibility to adapt strategies as needed.

Let's say that you make cookies. Collaborating with independent coffee shops or local markets puts your product in front of a new audience. In exchange, you can pay to rent shelf space or share a portion of your profits with the store. Check with your local chamber of commerce to find out what other businesses relevant to yours are in your area.[15]

Entering New Geographic Markets

Expanding to new places can help your business grow, but it's important to be smart about it. Before entering new markets, research what people there want and like. Check the local competition, but also consider things like infrastructure and legal requirements. Understand the risks, such as political issues or currency changes, and build strong local partnerships. To succeed, adjust your products, services, and how you market them to fit what people in that area are looking for. This demonstrates that you care about meeting their needs. Being thoughtful and adapting to local conditions increases the chances of success during expansion into new locations. And remember—just because a certain business succeeds in one local market, it doesn't necessarily mean that it will do so in another.

Mergers and Acquisitions

Mergers and acquisitions (M&A) occur either when two companies collaborate or when one entity acquires another. This can help businesses grow by expanding market share, diversifying products, or utilizing new technologies. However, it does come with challenges such as dealing with different cultures and associated financial risks. Successful M&A requires careful planning, determining if the companies match well, and smart integration after the deal. While it can be a powerful way for companies to grow quickly, it needs careful thinking, planning, and execution.

Franchising Your Business

Franchising is a reliable way to grow quickly, and it involves granting others (franchisees) permission to use your business model, brand, and assistance in return for fees and royalties. Start by assessing whether the franchising model aligns well with the structure of your S corporation. If so, create a thorough franchise strategy for success. Before moving forward, however, evaluate the scalability and replicability of your business model, ensuring that it can be readily replicated in diverse locations by various owners.

A comprehensive franchise strategy includes defining the franchise structure, fees, and terms. Provide clear guidelines on the use of your brand and business processes. Develop training programs to transfer your business knowledge to franchisees. Next, establish clear franchise terms, including fees, royalties, and support services. Provide training programs for franchisees to ensure that they understand and can replicate your business model effectively. It's crucial to create a strong brand identity and marketing strategy that franchisees can use to maintain consistency across locations.

Legal considerations are also essential in the franchising process. Work with legal professionals to develop franchise agreements and disclosure documents, and always comply with relevant regulations.

Franchising can be a lucrative way to grow, but success hinges on meticulous planning and execution. Assessing the suitability of your business model, creating standardized processes, and addressing legal aspects are key elements in building a successful franchise strategy.

A great example of a successful franchise is Five Guys Enterprises. It began as a local family restaurant—Five Guys Burgers and Fries—in

Arlington, VA and spent five years expanding into five locations around Washington, DC. The business grew organically and started to build a following. The owners looked into franchising in the nearest states to them, which became a wild success. Since 2003, the company has expanded to over 1,700 locations across the United States, Canada, United Kingdom, Europe, Asia, and the Middle East, with another 1,500 locations in development. This runaway success all started from a great concept, hard work, and smart growth.

Expanding Your Online Presence

The cornerstone of a robust online presence is a user-friendly website. Make certain that your website is easily navigable, delivers pertinent information, and provides visitors with a seamless experience. Also, ensure that you optimize it for search engines (SEO) to enhance visibility.

Moreover, establishing a strong and significant presence on social media platforms is crucial for reaching and engaging with a broader audience. Identify the platforms most pertinent to your target audience, and then generate compelling content that encourages interaction. Social media serves as a valuable channel for marketing, customer service, and cultivating brand awareness, and it's an area that cannot be overlooked.

Maintaining consistency is essential when broadening your online presence. Ensure regular updates of your website with fresh content, and sustain an active, engaging presence on social media. Respond promptly to customer inquiries and actively participate in relevant conversations within your industry. Overall, by focusing on both a user-friendly website and a strong social media presence, you can effectively expand your online presence, connect with your audience, and remain competitive in the digital landscape.

Funding Options for Growth

When aiming to scale your business, it's vital to consider different funding options to support your growth initiatives. Two primary avenues in this regard are attracting investors and venture capital, as well as exploring small business loans and financing.

Attracting investors and venture capital involves seeking financial support from individuals or investment firms interested in your business. Investors commonly contribute funds in exchange for equity or ownership stakes in your company. Venture capital is a distinct form of investment in which professional groups invest in high-potential startups or expanding businesses in return for equity.

On the other hand, small business loans and financing involve borrowing money to fuel your expansion, which can be obtained from banks, financial institutions, or online lenders. Small business loans come with various terms and interest rates, and they require repayment over time.

Prior to selecting a funding option, thoroughly evaluate your business requirements, financial position, and growth strategies. Each funding method comes with its advantages and disadvantages, making it crucial to choose the one that aligns with your business goals and financial capabilities.

You can also choose to bootstrap your business, which simply means that you fund it from your savings. The advantage here is that it allows you to maintain 100% control of the business and equity. The disadvantage, however, is that it can be more risky. It can potentially lead to even more cash flow issues, especially early on when more capital is required and you have yet to make any significant sales.

Leveraging Social Media Marketing to Grow Your S Corp

Social media marketing is a sign of our times, and it offers platforms with which to connect with a broad audience and effectively engage potential customers.

There are a myriad of platforms you can focus on, but the ones that most businesses utilize are YouTube, Instagram, and TikTok, which all offer the fastest opportunity for growth. The beauty of these platforms is that short-form content has exploded. The right kinds of 30 to 60-second videos can significantly grow your reach and bring in new customers.

This is an opportunity that simply wasn't around five or 10 years ago. If you wanted to blow up and expand your reach on social media in those days, you mostly had to put a painstaking amount of work into creating long-form content on YouTube. But with YouTube Shorts, Instagram Reels, and TikTok, this is no longer the case.

Businesses are quickly growing their accounts by hundreds of thousands of potential customers—sometimes in the span of just a few months—with the right short-form content that resonates with their audience. It's a rapid way to boost brand visibility and attract new customers. In addition, it's incredibly cost effective, as it involves attracting organic traffic.

Tips for Short-Form Social Media Content to Attract Business

The following are some tips to build your business' following—and attract buyers—on these social media platforms:

1. **Start with a Hook:** You want to engage your viewers quickly by

capturing their attention straight away. For example, you can ask a compelling question like, "What if I told you there's a simple way to…"

2. **Keep it Short:** Ensure that your videos are concise but punchy. Think "all meat and no fluff."

3. **Use Trends and Hashtags:** Join popular challenges, use relevant hashtags, and feature trending music in your content.

4. **Show Products Creatively:** Present your products or services in a creative and visually enticing manner. (A business that does this seamlessly is GymShark, an athletic clothing brand, which has been able to amass over five million followers on TikTok.)

5. **Be Authentic:** People appreciate authenticity, so make sure that you're genuine. Sharing behind-the-scenes moments is a great tactic. (If you run an e-commerce brand, you could show some "backstage" content from the warehouse or the office where you're creatively planning your next awesome product.)

6. **Engage with Your Audience:** Interact with users and messages to establish a community around your brand. Aim to respond to as many comments as possible.

7. **Post Regularly:** Maintaining consistency is crucial, so ensure that you're regularly sharing content to remain on your audience's radar. When it comes to short-form content, the minimum you'll want to pose is once per day if you really want to grow.

8. **Experiment with Styles:** Play around with various content styles to discover what resonates most effectively with your audience. If something flops, try a new angle.

9. **Include a Call-to-Action (CTA):** Encourage viewers to take action, such as sending you a direct message, visiting your website, or buying a product.

A fantastic advantage of short-form content is that you can film a content piece once, and then post on TikTok, Instagram Reels, and YouTube shorts. In this way, that piece of content potentially has three times as much reach.

Below are a few accounts you can follow for more in-depth strategies on growing with short-form content:

Instacoach Mike: https://www.instagram.com/instacoachmike

Viral Video Club: https://www.instagram.com/viralvideo.club

Brock Johnson: https://www.instagram.com/brock11johnson

The YouTube Strategy

Explore the idea of creating longer-form videos on YouTube when you need to provide more in-depth content or tutorials. This versatile platform allows for a mix of short and extended content, offering the flexibility to dive deep into topics that require more time and explanation.

Longer videos are particularly effective for creating tutorials, educational content, and engaging storytelling that can build brand identity. By utilizing YouTube, businesses can position themselves as authorities in their industries, as well as connect with audiences on a deeper level. Additionally, longer videos may open the doors to monetization opportunities, such as ads, sponsorships, or participation in the YouTube Partner Program, contributing to potential revenue generation.

Striking a balance between short- and long-form content on YouTube ensures a well-rounded and engaging presence for businesses seeking to connect with their audience through diverse content formats. Think of it this way: Short-form content is like promoting your business, and long-form YouTube content is nurturing and indoctrinating those who've found you through short-form content. Longer pieces of content allow you to build trust in a way that's harder to do with purely short-form content.

X (formerly known as Twitter) Strategies

Leverage X for providing real-time updates, prompting engaging conversations, and building a community around your brand. X is a dynamic platform on which timely communication is key. Share up-to-the-moment updates about your business, industry trends, and relevant news. You can interact with your audience through conversations, respond to comments, and join relevant discussions.

Establishing a community on X entails cultivating a sense of connection and belonging among your followers. Encourage user-generated content, conduct polls, and host Xchats to boost engagement. X can be leveraged as a powerful tool for brand promotion and connecting with your audience. A great account to follow on X is Nick Huber (https://twitter.com/sweatystartup). He's launched several companies via X, and he uses his account to tweet relevant business advice and bring in more customers to these different businesses.

Scaling with Ads

Scaling your business involves a strategic use of advertising, as well as understanding the basics of key channels. Social media ads on platforms like Facebook, X, Instagram, TikTok, and LinkedIn offer targeted approaches. Define your audience parameters, set clear campaign goals, and craft compelling ad content to engage your target demographic. There's a decent likelihood that you're not an ads expert (if you are, you've got a leg up!). Your business may not be big enough to hire a full-time ads expert either, and you likely don't have the time to learn all the ins and outs of what it takes to run successful ads yourself. This is why it's usually best to bring on a contractor to get your ads up and running, but it's imperative that you know exactly what you're trying to accomplish with them. Are you interested in expanding your reach? Selling products? Determining what you're aiming to do with your ads is critical from the outset, as it avoids mixed signals and inconsistencies in your message.

Once you know your goals, you can work with an experienced contractor to decide on the best platforms and types of ads with which to scale your business to the next level. Usually, this will comprise a mix of social media ads along with Google ads as well.

Influencer Marketing

Unlock the potential of influencer marketing by collaborating with influencers whose values resonate with your brand. Influencers can play a crucial role in promoting your products or services to their followers, providing valuable exposure and enhancing credibility.

Identify influencers whose audience demographics align with your target market, and establish authentic partnerships with them. This approach capitalizes on the authenticity of the influencer to establish a more genuine connection with your audience, thereby contributing to the overall success of your marketing endeavors.

Let's consider men's skincare company Tiege Hanley as an example. It identified where its target market (men between 18 and 50) hangs out online. The company realized that there was a big crossover with male influencers in niches like dating and style advice, as well as overall self-improvement for men.

After discovering this, Tiege Hanley decided to focus heavily on teaming up with these male influencers, which allowed the company to scale up and dramatically expand its reach. It's getting harder to find a male self-improvement influencer who hasn't promoted Tiege Hanley. By tapping into the power of influencers, the company's brand awareness has skyrocketed.

Strategies for Working with Influencers to Promote Your Brand (and What You Can Expect)

When partnering with influencers, it's crucial to have a clear strategy. Define your expectations, goals, and metrics for success. Influencers can significantly impact your brand, so choose your collaborations wisely.

As touched upon above, select influencers whose audience aligns with your target market and shares similar values. Expect them to bring authenticity and a unique touch to your brand, leading to increased visibility and credibility. Select who you'd like to work with carefully by considering factors like reputation and relevance. Once the collaboration has begun, regularly assess performance using defined metrics to ensure that your goals are met. A well-implemented influencer marketing strategy has the potential to significantly enhance the promotion of your product or brand and bring your company to soaring new heights.

Key Takeaways

1. Market research is used to identify trends, customer preferences, and growth opportunities, as well as to determine how to stand out and be adaptable to market changes.

2. To attract a wide customer base, diversify your product or service offerings.

3. Strategic partnerships and alliances can increase revenue, reach more customers, and help you to stay competitive.

4. Expanding into new geographic markets can be accomplished by tailoring your products, services, and marketing strategies to suit local needs.

5. Franchising can scale and replicate your business model into diverse and previously uncharted markets.

6. Funding factors for growth include investors, venture capitalists, small business loans, and other forms of financing.

7. Developing an online presence includes crafting a user-friendly website optimized for search engines and a strong, compelling presence on social media platforms.

Conclusion

Whether you're still in the planning stages or well into your business journey, navigating the tricky waters of an S corporation is both challenging and rewarding. Throughout this book, we've presented you with a myriad of helpful information, **including:**

- The advantages and drawbacks of the S corporation structure

- How to establish and qualify for an S corporation

- Choosing board members and shareholders

- The best place to set up your location

- How to negotiate with suppliers and vendors

- The ins and outs of hiring and paying employees

- Establishing and maintaining your accounting system

- Ensuring adherence with federal and local rules and regulations

- How to grow, scale, and even sell your business

While we've provided a comprehensive guide covering many aspects of an S corporation, you'll undoubtedly still have some questions that are specific to your particular industry or locality. We encourage you to consult professionals—lawyers, accountants, tax experts, and other business owners—to ensure that you're in compliance. On the following pages, you'll find a list of many organizations that can help.

Equipped with the tools, tips, and techniques presented in these pages, we believe that you're now well-prepared to embark on the next phase of business ownership.

If you found value in this book, kindly consider leaving a review on Amazon. We're certain that there are individuals just like you who could use a push in the right direction in forming their S corporation. As they say, knowledge is power, and it's our hope that we've armed you sufficiently for your journey ahead.

A Parting Gift

As a way of saying thank you for your purchase, we're giving you our *"7-Figure Business Toolkit"* that includes five FREE downloads that are exclusive to our book readers!

Here's what you'll get:

6. **The Negotiation Mastery Cheat Sheet** – Master the art of negotiation and get a massive edge in your business.

7. **The Start Your LLC Checklist** – This step-by-step PDF shows you exactly how to get your LLC up and running right away.

8. **The Top 7 Websites To Start Your LLC** – Save hours on research and choose the best website to start your LLC.

9. **The Mindfulness Hacks for Entrepreneurs PDF** – Stay cool, calm, and collected through all the ups and downs of your business journey.

10. **The 5 Mistakes Beginners Make When Opening an LLC** – An email course that helps you avoid the most COSTLY mistakes when getting started.

To download your 7-Figure Business Toolkit, you can go to

https://llclegend.com/llc-s-corp-bonus **or simply scan the QR code below:**

Can You Do Us a Favor?

Thanks for checking out our book.

We're confident this will help you build your LLC and create a thriving business!

Would you take 60 seconds and write a quick blurb about this book on Amazon?

Reviews are the best way for independent authors (like us) to get noticed, sell more books, and spread our message to as many people as possible. We also read every review and use the feedback to write future revisions – and future books, even.

You can leave a review at the below URL or scan the QR code:

mybook.to/LLC-bundle

Thank you – we really appreciate your support.

About the Author

Garrett Monroe is a pen name for a team of writers with business experience in various industries, like coaching, sales, AI, real estate, copywriting, accounting, etc. They've built teams, understand how to manage people, and know what it takes to be a successful entrepreneur. These writers have come together to share their knowledge and produce a series of business books and help you take your business endeavors to the next level.

References

Chapter 1 - S Corporations

1. https://www.irs.gov/businesses/small-businesses-self-employed/s-corporations The IRS website is where you'll find forms and explanations of what's required of an S corporation.

2. https://www.sba.gov/business-guide/launch-your-business/register-your-business The Small Business Association is a local and national organization that connects entrepreneurs with lenders and funding to help them plan, start, and grow their business.

Chapter 2 - Formation

1. https://www.sba.gov/business-guide/launch-your-business/apply-licenses-permits The Small Business Administration can also help with required licenses and permits.

2. https://s-corp.org/about/ This Washington, D.C.-based organization defends the rights of S corporations, and it'sa great resource for keeping up with changing laws.

Chapter 3 - Accounting

1. https://us.aicpa.org/advocacy/tax/scorporationsThe Association of International Certified Personal Accountants focuses on accounting principles, including those that affect your S corporation.

Chapter 4 - Taxes

1. https://www.irs.gov/newsroom/qualified-business-income-deductionThe IRS website has information on deductions for taxes.

2. https://forum.whitecoatinvestor.com/tax-reduction/321748-questions-on-creating-an-s-corporationForums such as this one are crucial to keep informed of changes in S corporation compliance and laws.

Chapter 5 - Financial

1. https://www.sbdcnet.org/find-your-local-sbdc-office/Your local Small Business Development Center (SBDC) provides counseling and training to small businesses and entrepreneurs in areas such as capital, technology, planning, strategy, operations, and more.

2. https://www.score.org/A stand-alone division of the SBA, SCORE offers mentoring, webinars, courses, guides, templates, videos, and more to help small business owners and entrepreneurs succeed.

Chapter 6 - Bookkeeping

1. https://nacpb.org/free-bookkeeper-resources/The National Association of Certified Public Bookkeepers has free resources you'll find essential if you're acting as your own bookkeeper.

Chapter 7 - Payroll and People

1. https://www.usa.gov/labor-lawsA resource on the official website of the US Government offering information on labor laws.

2. https://www.irs.gov/forms-pubs/about-form-1120-sThe IRS website has all the forms you need to file your taxes.

Chapter 8 - Compliance

1. https://www.nfib.com/The National Federation of Independent Business (NFIB) is a non-profit organization that advocates on behalf of small and independent business owners in all 50 states and Washington, D.C.

Chapter 9 - Scaling Your Business Online Presence/Social Media

1. https://www.bni.com/Organizations such as Business Networking International (BNI) are a great place to meet like-minded business professionals.

2. https://www.chamberofcommerce.com/Your local chamber of commerce provides opportunities to promote your business in your jurisdiction. This website is an international directory of businesses, but a quick search of your town and the words "chamber of commerce" will generally put you in touch with your local group.

Made in the USA
Middletown, DE
01 September 2024

60167513R00176